Wanderings

over

Bible Lands and Seas.

By the Author of

THE SCHÖNBERG-COTTA FAMILY.

1. THE TWO VOCATIONS. A Tale. $1 25
"The Two Vocations is a new work by the author of 'The Schonberg-Cotta Family,' being, unlike most of her earlier works, a story of modern life, and adapted to juvenile readers. It traces the religious history of two bright little girls from childhood to maturity; girls differing widely in tastes and talents, yet each led by the discipline of events to a beneficent vocation. The book is an earnest one, of deep religious interest, and well fitted for a young girl's library."—*Springfield Republican.*

2. TALES OF CHRISTIAN LIFE. 16mo. 1 25
"The tales are painted in such an inimitable manner that while they interest and attract, they impart much historical information, and they are pervaded by the heroic spirit of Christianity. They should be in all Sabbath-schools."—*Baptist Quarterly.*

3. THE MARTYRS OF SPAIN. 1 25
"The author, who has thrown so much fascination over the history of Luther, in the great work of Reformation, has adopted the same plan in illustrating anew the fierce and relentless persecution in Spain against the Protestants."—*Presbyterian.*

4. THE CRIPPLE OF ANTIOCH. 1 25
These sketches present vivid pictures of life among the early Christians in the generation immediately following the apostolic days.

5. THE VOICE OF CHRISTIAN LIFE IN SONG In many Lands and Ages. Red Edges. 1 50

6. THE THREE WAKINGS, and other Poems. Red Edges. 1 25

7. THE BLACK SHIP, and other Allegories. 18mo. 90

8. WANDERINGS OVER BIBLE LANDS.

Bible Lands.

A Scene in the South of Palestine.

FRONTISPIECE.

Wanderings

over

Bible Lands and Seas.

By the Author of the
"SCHÖNBERG-COTTA FAMILY."

NEW-YORK:
ROBERT CARTER & BROTHERS,
530 Broadway.
1866.

CONTENTS.

Wanderings Over

Bible Lands and Seas.

I.

Malta.

* * * *

Thursday, off Malta.

AT seven on Tuesday morning we went on shore and climbed the steep streets of Valetta. Immediately after breakfast in the Imperial Hotel we took a carriage with a pair of small Maltese horses, and drove to Citta Vecchia in the interior. Malta is the most dazzling, barren place you can conceive. Imagine Dartmoor without one stream, without gorse or heather, with the short grass burnt up, and dazzling, light brown earth showing through; every hundred yards walls of loose stones of the same dazzling tint crossing each other. Occasionally you pass a field of barley looking a dry, dull green, with square stone buildings in the middle of the fields covering wells. Twice we crossed rocky hollows which looked like water-courses, and in these some dusty, thirsty-looking trees and shrubs were growing, but not a drop of water trickled there. Every now and then we came to a high ground, and saw the intense blue sea, stretching from bay to bay, the low brown points of land running some miles out. In the stone walls there are no gates, only gaps filled up roughly with loose stones. Everywhere, in houses, soil, hedges, roads; through the thin, dry vegetation, glares the same dazzling rock, the color of Maltese vases. The flat roofs of the houses made them at a distance look like ruins, to our unaccustomed English eyes.

* * * *

On Wednesday morning we drove to St.

Paul's Bay, having satisfied ourselves from Mr. Smith's book that it really was the scene of St. Paul's shipwreck. Therefore we could quietly listen to the stories of our guides about the chapel built on the very spot where the barbarians lighted the fire, and St. Paul shook off the viper. It is at least refreshing to have traditions so near the truth as these, instead of legends of eleven thousand virgins and mediæval nuns and monks. It does thrill one's heart to hear even the name of that noble apostle honored.

It is intensely interesting thus to come within the range of Bible history and geography with our bodily eyes,—to see the scenes apostles saw, to have all the sights and sounds, the very stars, and seas, and shores, which made their visible heavens and earth audibly and visibly around us. Superstition fondly treasures the dead relics of the past—some poor crumbling bone of the body. God watches over and will raise incorruptible, some spot of dust on which holy feet have trod. Faith revivifies the past by a community of life with those who lived in it; "they are not dead, but living, for all live unto Him." To our *faith* Hudson's Bay, of which apostles never heard, is as holy as the Sea of Galilee; and the streets of London, which Christians tread, as sacred as the streets of Jerusalem, "where our Lord was crucified,"—because the tread of those blessed feet has consecrated the whole earth, if any part of it, and the majesty of that living Presence fills the whole universe. The least blade of grass which pierces the clods to-day with its green tapering spear is sacred with the touch of His hand; the waves of the Mediterranean are consecrated because His present power curves and crisps them to-day, not because St. Paul was shipwrecked by them eighteen hundred years ago. But our religion is a religion of *facts* as well as *truths*,—a history of things which have been done, as well as a revelation of unseen realities which are eternal; and it is this which gives the undying interest to Eastern travel.

St. Paul, a *man* who suffered and rejoiced

as well as a prophet of immortal truth,—a man who, centuries since, was shipwrecked among the rocks at the entrance of this bay now called by his name, was drifted on a broken plank through *those* waves, then dashing wildly in the storm, to *this* low, sandy, shelving beach at the head of the bay, and so escaped safe to *this* shore; and it does help our imagination, and may strengthen our faith, to stand here and see and feel how his natural world—his body, with its dangers and wants—was the very same as ours, just as his heart, and the truths which warmed and fed it, were the same. The bay seems nearly to close at the entrance, which is sheltered by two rocky headlands which look like islands, but are joined by a low ridge to the shore. The shores are in some places precipitous, in others sloping, in all bare and rocky, except at the head of the bay, which is a sandy beach or "shore." The rocky, almost isolated headland at the entrance breaks the currents and tides, and must cause eddies where the two seas—the divided and recoiling waves—rush round and "meet" again. There, near that headland, they had run the ship aground, and the waves were still dashing against the wreck and breaking it in pieces, while the shipwrecked men, tossed one by one on the beach, stood shivering on the wet sands, the rain pouring on them, and no shelter in sight.

They must have begun to know St. Paul by this time; he had encouraged them to take their last meal before the Egyptian wheat, which made their cargo, was thrown into the sea. They knew that he had a God in whom he trusted, and who spoke to him, and had told him the truth. They had seen him give thanks before any hope of safety appeared. The centurion had learned to value him, and preferred the risk of the escape of all the other prisoners to the risk of not saving Paul. And now, of all the soldiers and sailors, men inured to hardships, it was Paul—"Paul the aged" who gathered the bundle of sticks among those low bushes in the valley, and laid them on the fire. Fancy St. Paul stirring busily about in the rain, gathering firewood for that shivering, despondent crew. In its way, I would as soon have seen that as have heard him preach on the Areopagus. The faith which had made him sublimely courageous in the great peril made him cheerful and helpful in little difficulties; and that faith makes him grander in a Christian's eyes than the miracle which so soon afterwards made him seem a god to those poor, kindly islanders. They had certainly never seen any so like God before, as he went in and out before them, healing rich and poor. Many races in their migration westward have paused on Malta since then,—Roman colonists, Arab and Crusading knights; but the name of the shipwrecked Jewish prisoner is still honored there. Can we not feel how they must have clung to the stranger who brought such blessings with him, free alike to the Roman colonists and the barbarous people. What the religion of the islanders was we know not; they certainly believed in an avenging power which pursued crime, and surely in his three months' sojourn the apostle taught them of the redeeming love which forgives sin, and of the atoning sacrifice which takes it away. They knew that sin brings misery; surely he did not fail to tell them of Him whose precious blood and redeeming death blots out sin. They thought of crime as an indelible stain only to be outstained by a deeper stain of vengeance; surely he told them of the precious blood which can wash out that indelible stain, and make the crimson white as snow.

One would like to know how the apostle, who met the Stoics and Epicureans on their own ground, and Pharisees on theirs, spoke to these barbarians. What a model for missionaries to the South Seas and all uncivilized tribes! But the Bible does not give us model sermons; it gives us living truths, to live first in our hearts, and thence be sown in those of others. No variety of models could suit our infinite variety of circumstances, but life adapts itself to all. And so after those three months of honors and courteous hospitality, with the whole crew laden with necessaries, (no doubt for his sake,) the apostle patiently left, in another Alexandrian ship, again a prisoner, calmly giving himself up to imprisonment and martyrdom, or rather, as we know from his own words, joyfully going forth to the crown of glory, and to the Lord who gives it.

After this the knights of Malta seem very modern and secular, but their noble struggle with the Turks is the next event of world-wide interest in the history of Malta. In the afternoon, after seeing St. Paul's Bay, we took a boat and rowed across the Grand Harbor to the old city, which, from the brave and victorious defence the knights made of it, was called afterwards Vittoriosa. You remember Prescott's narrative of the siege in his Philip the Second. After the Turks were finally driven off, the Grand Master, La Valette, the hero of the siege, built Valetta on the opposite side of the harbor to that on which the old city stood, on the tongue of land between the Quarantine Harbor, where our ship lay, and the Grand Harbor. The old Fort of St. Elmo, so gallantly defended by its little isolated garrison of knights, stood on the point of this tongue of land, (then unpeopled, now the city of Valetta,) and it was from that point that the messenger swam across the Grand Harbor, by the Turkish fleet, to the great Fort of St. Angelo, close to Vittoriosa. We went over the Fort of St. Angelo, saw the old chapel of the knights (now an armory,) and the prison where the Turkish prisoners were kept. We looked from the battlements where the knights watched so often vainly for succor.

* * * *

Now we are again at sea,—Malta vanishing into a faint haze in the distance. It is strange to look at it and think of the two points in its history which stand out illuminated from the obscurity or common place of the rest. The first gives us a brief glimpse of it in the light which the Bible throws around the infancy of the Church, and shows us its inhabitants, simple, courteous, kindly, suffering from various diseases, and in terror of avenging superhuman powers,—the shipwrecked apostle, out of weakness made strong, bringing healing and blessing with him because he had communion with superhuman redeeming love.

The next salient point in Maltese history, fifteen centuries after, shows us the ascetic misrepresentation of the Christianity St. Paul preached run to seed in the military monastic order of the Hospitallers, and yet, even in such decay, nobler than anything else the world had to offer, and strong enough by endurance and daring valor to keep at bay the whole Mohammedan power.

II.

Egypt.

CAIRO, May 22.

EGYPT is *not*, as the old woman thought, a place somewhere between the earth and sky. We are treading its soil, and breathing its air, with no Lethe between us and you. God's parables are written on actual places, and in real histories. . . . .

It is Ramadan, the great Mohammedan fast, and numbers of Mussulmen were going through their prostrations in each mosque we visited, whilst many more were stretched out asleep in the shade. They are glad to forget the fast in sleep, until the sunset gun gives them permission to seek the happier oblivion of the pipe. How deeply this idea of self-denial for the sake of self-denial is ingrained in most false religions! In Christianity only the true root is reached, and self-sacrifice is honored but as the fruit of love. "Who *loved* me and gave himself for me," is the keynote of Christian self-denial.

The mosque of the Sultan Hassan is the most interesting we saw; the concave, shell-like Moorish carving of the roof and porch, and ornamental Arabic inscriptions, are really beautiful. But all is ruinous; birds building nests in the decayed roof of the fountain, the richly carved wooden lattices and fret-work broken, and the delicate yet gorgeous painting and gilding worn off. Mohammedanism also had its golden age of art, contemporary with that of Gothic architecture, but its inspiration seems to have been rather from the genius of a race than the enthusiasm of a religion. Moslem art is not Mohammedan, but Moorish, and with the Moors and their caliphates it died away. Mohammedanism proclaimed a truth which gave it a temporary force; it had no life to renew the impulse when its first force grew feeble. The mosques at Cairo are strangely typical of the religion. Contrasted with the dark, encumbered Greek and Coptic churches, with their narrow divisions between clergy and laity and their wretched ornaments, there is something very grand and impressive about the great spaces of the mosques. You feel they are built in honor of the Unseen and Eternal, and that the worship offered there at least recognises an invisible power. But it is only power—irresistible, inaccessible power. The name of Allah is scarcely more than a personification of destiny; and there is a melancholy appropriateness in the worship of destiny amidst ruined temples. What, indeed, is ruin but the impress of the iron hand of their deity? It is said that the Moslems think it sacrilege to repair what the hand of fate has stamped with decay. Therefore the beautiful old Moorish mosques, costly in materials, gorgeous in coloring, and delicate in workmanship, are left to decay, whilst, beside them, rises the tasteless modern building with its common materials, tinsel ornament, and coarse workmanship. . .

ANCIENT EGYPT.

The road to the Pyramids, sandy and dry, led between stubbly fields, and was bordered by ditches, overgrown with tall reeds and flags—so tall as to throw quite a shadow across the road, yet so slender that the lightest wind might shake them, so as to "bruise" them, and it must indeed be a gentle touch which would not break one so "bruised." Every now and then we passed through large groves, or rather forests of palms; their beautiful queenly plumes waved high above us in the breeze which did not descend to us, and their symmetrical giant stems were regularly knotted like the sculpture of a Moorish roof. For miles after we first caught sight of the Pyramids, we rode directly towards them, keeping them full in view along all that straight road across the level land, watching them gradually enlarge until they filled the field of vision, and so, slowly, we grew to feel their size.....

From the top of the Pyramids the whole

Bible land of Egypt lay spread before us,—Goshen, On (the buried priestly city where Moses studied), the fields where the Hebrews toiled despairingly, the river where the babe lay among the bulrushes,—all that strange, familiar land of the Great River, between the glowing sands of the Arabian desert, and the Libyan desert, on the edge of which we stood. We looked over the sand-wastes, over the tombs partly disinterred from among them, over the Great Sphinx at our feet, across the green valley of the Nile with its palm-forests, and across white Cairo with its pearly minarets, to the sand wastes on the other side of Egypt, and the Mokattam hills which bound the Eastern horizon—the hills through a pass of which Israel went forth to their miraculous crossing of the Red Sea. All this lay far beneath us, silent as the dead generations who had dwelt there, or as if it had been a vision evoked from the past to illustrate the Scripture history.

To-day (Friday), after a day's rest, we started at five on our donkeys, and breakfasted on cold tea, bread, and apricots, in a fruit garden at the foot of the solitary obelisk which is all that remains of Heliopolis, the sacred city, the On, where Joseph's wife, Asenath, lived. A few scattered blocks, one in the form of a trough, another of an altar of libation, one of which is covered with hieroglyphics, clear as if cut yesterday—these, with some mounds of sand and rubbish, are all the traces of the magnificent priestly city now left to mark its site.

Near this obelisk is a very large ancient well, from which two oxen were drawing up the water by means of wheels and ropes with buckets attached to them. The water which poured from these buckets formed quite a copious stream, and was beautifully clear and sweet. This is called the Well of Sitti Mariam (my Lady Mary.) The tradition of the native Christians is that the Virgin mother drank of it in the flight into Egypt, and from a bitter fountain it at once became sweet. Close to this well, in a garden of pomegranates, roses, syringa, and fruit trees, is a magnificent old sycamore, under the shade of which they say the Virgin rested with the infant Saviour. Precise places are of little moment to us, or they would have been precisely revealed, but it did seem to bring Him very near, the ever-living Lord, who was once indeed a little child, to think that on these very scenes his infant eyes did really rest. For this part of Egypt—the same undoubtedly where Joseph lived, where the Israelites toiled in hard bondage, and where Moses was found by Pharaoh's daughter on the river—contained long after the Christian era, a colony of Jews, and would most probably have been the district Joseph and Mary would have chosen for a refuge. This very district is, they say, unquestionably the scene of the various Scripture narratives about Egypt; that is, the region round Cairo, and from Cairo to Alexandria and the sea, interlaced with the mouths of the Nile. To Memphis, the Scriptural Noph, we are going to-morrow; in Heliopolis, Joseph's On, we rested to-day, and on the Pyramids probably Abraham looked. After these, the tombs of the Mameluke kings, with their rich Mosaic marbles, sculptured roofs and porches, Moorish arches, ornamented domes, and delicately fretted minarets, had a very cold interest for us, in spite of the impress of Mohammed's foot in marble exhibited there. But it was interesting to hear the muezzin call from the minaret to noon-day prayer, "Allah el Allah—God is God, and Mohammed is the prophet of God." That solitary voice on high, amidst these silent deserts, or piercing the din of the city at mid-day, has a strangely solemn sound. Amongst the people, however, the name of God seems little more than an emphatic particle; in calling one another, scolding, unlading waggons, driving donkeys, it is perpetually "Allah," "Meshallah," "Inshallah," "Wallah." We passed the Turkish cemetery on our way back to Cairo, a dreary, hopeless looking place, white headstones scattered about it, and occasionally a turban sculptured on them.

In the evening we started at eight o'clock for Boulac on the Nile, on our way to the ancient Memphis. It was dark when we reached Boulac. The minarets were illuminated, and the Ramadan fast being over for the day, picturesque groups were sitting in the streets, smoking, drinking sherbet and coffee, listening to singers or musicians playing monotonous minor airs, gathering attentively round a story-teller, or playing chess; but no family groups, nothing to indicate the existence of *homes*. For picturesqueness of costume there is nothing like the East, the flow of the drapery so simple and natural, the coloring so deep and brilliant, the attitudes so calm and dignified—no vulgarity because no pretence. If these human beings were only figures in the landscape, the harmony of man and nature would certainly be more complete here than anywhere; but since the landscape is only an accessory to human life, and those picturesque figures are human and immortal, the thought of their

An Egyptian Scene.

p. 28.

life does weigh often very heavily on the heart.

Our Nile boat was ready for us when we reached the river; the Rais welcomed us courteously. There was a long, narrow, half-deck, with chairs on it, and three rooms opening from it, the two outer ones with sofas on each side, the inner one all one cushioned divan, into which, (having heard that the Mecca pilgrims often use these boats,) we did not venture to enter. We watched the glorious clear stars till late from the deck, and then retired to sleep on the sofas. Once we looked out through the Venetian shutters, and saw the moonlight on the Nile. About two in the morning we reached Bedrasheen, and at daybreak we started on donkeys for the Sakhara Pyramids.

We reached Memphis, after a delicious cool breezy ride among the green maize fields and palm forests. An Arab woman, strange to say, showed us over the pits and mounds which mark the ruins, all the men of the village being absent. The fallen colossus of Rameses the king is most impressive; it lies on its side among the great weeds as if reposing, the placid giant face quietly smiling at fate. From the chin to the top of the forehead it measures seven feet; complete, it stood fifty feet high. Many smaller fragments and remains lie around, one or two perfect sitting figures, a few heads and feet, and some blocks covered with hieroglyphics. But the ruin is indeed most utter, the desolation complete. The ruins of two wretched Arab mud villages close at hand make more show than those of that great city. These Lybian Bedouin abandon their mud huts, and retire with their herds and flocks to the desert on the slightest disturbance. Indeed, their huts are scarcely more settled habitations than tents.

From Memphis we rode to the Sakhara Pyramids on the Lybian sand desert, close to the village of Abousir. We were not in the least prepared for what we saw there. The Serapium, the great crypt or vault of the bull-god Apis, is most wonderful; an enormous subterranean vaulted nave with forty side chambers (like the side chapels of a cathedral), each containing a colossal sarcophagus of granite or black marble for the body of the dead Apis. The lids have been pushed back, and every tomb rifled. Each sarcophagus, with the lid, is about twelve feet high, and of great thickness. The Bedouin guide and Gabriel, our dragoman, carried two candles each; and the effects of light and shade on the vaulted rock-roof, and the black arched recesses with their enormous sarcophaguses, each of which was once walled in, were most weird and strange. Neither drawing nor description can give an idea of it. The great characteristic is size, and the mysterious depths of the recesses even Rembrandt could only give in fragments. But the whole of these gigantic traces of the animal worship, under whose shadow the Israelites had groaned so long, enable one better to understand Aaron's golden calf, and the "these be thy gods, O Israel;" and Moses' dread of sacrificing in their sight the abomination of the Egyptians.

The temple of Phtha (the Egypt Vulcan) was another subterranean wonder. Irregular rock pillars support the cavernous roof, the outer chambers lead you to the inner shrine, whose walls are covered with hieroglyphics. A painted altar stands at the inmost end, and pits, which were tombs, lie rifled around.

After this we visited the ibis-pits, long winding galleries excavated in the rock, honeycombing the hills. They contain earthen jars by thousands, each one protecting its ibis mummy, although now you must penetrate very far to find one. Our Bedouin guide dived into the far recesses and extracted one for us. We broke it open and discovered the mummy in its linen wrappings, which we intend to bring home. The whole region is honeycombed with tombs of the sacred beasts. Sakhara was the quarter for the tombs of the gods, as

Ghizeh was for the tombs of the kings. We saw a hyena prowling about among the sand hills, and, soon after, we set out homewards or boatwards under the burning sun, dismounting from our donkeys on the way, to rest and take luncheon under the shade of a twin palm-tree.

The wind was quite against us on our way back; our boatmen, therefore, had to row, and as one of them was twice as strong as the other, and kept pulling him round, the voyage was performed in a series of zigzags. When we could keep sufficiently near the shore, one of the men waded in the mud and dragged us on by a rope. They encouraged each other with strange, wild, monotonous songs; invocations to Allah, and strings of his titles continually recurring in the same constantly repeated, mournful nasal minor chant. When the sunset gun from the citadel of Cairo announced that the day's fast was over, they laid aside their oars, washed their hands and faces in the river (muttering, we thought, some prayers as they did so), ate some bread, and began to smoke. It was indeed most impressive to see the power maintained for centuries by the word and will of a dead man. For us, then, what should be the power of the word of a living God,—God manifest in the flesh?

The journey was not wearisome, intense as the heat was; and it was worth lingering to see the sunset from the Nile. From our low boat from the low state of the river we could see nothing but the high mud banks, marked by the terraces made by the Nile as it rises, that is, we could see nothing of the nearer shores—the middle distance was entirely lost—but on one side, in the further distance, the pyramids of Ghizeh rose like conical hills against the sunset, and on the bank itself we saw a troop of camels, donkeys, sheep, and goats, each figure pencilled as if with the most delicate miniature brush against the golden sky. Beyond these at times rose a palm grove, each tree in the same delicate and exquisite relief; whilst on the other side the beautiful rose and violet tints colored the hills and quarries of Masara, throwing out in perfect distinctness the square cuttings from which the stones of the buried and desolate Noph and On were taken.

Sunday.—We had a pleasant English service at the missionary church. Mr. Lieder gave us a beautiful meditation on the sufferings of our Lord in his humanity to enable him to sympathize with us. Mr. and Mrs. Lieder are very kind to us. I believe many travelers have much reason to be grateful to them. Mr. Lieder has every evening a class of young men and boys who come to read the Arabic Bible. Mrs. Lieder has a school for Coptic, Armenian, Syrian, and Turkish girls. I saw them last week. Their costumes and countenances were very varied and interesting; some were just like those on the old Egyptian tombs, the braided silk head-pendent twisted with gold coins, the eyelids dyed black with kohl, and the nails and palms of the hands stained pink with henna. It was strange to see the forms so familiar in stone translated into hair, and silk, and flesh. Many of these girls had intelligent, nice faces; but until the harem system is broken down, the missionaries seem to think little or nothing can be done. The native Christians, Copts, &c., copy the Mussulmen in the seclusion of the women. For instance, a bright, intelligent, well-instructed girl from this school married a Copt the other day, and she must not leave her two upper rooms for a year at least! Meantime, what becomes of what she has learned? In the evening we had a refreshing, quiet service at the American mission house. This mission is but recently commenced, but here also there is a school.

I shall always be most thankful for this journey. It has given us such a glimpse into Oriental customs and into missionary life, its dangers and temptations, as well as its work. One is so apt to think of missionaries as of men necessarily on a higher level than ordinary Christians. The step of voluntary exile for Christ's sake seems to carry them into a higher sphere. But we should remember that the Christian race is not accomplished in great steps. The great enemy goes with the missionaries; the old man is within them; the world meets them everywhere in new disguises; the terrible deadening shadow of absolute heathenism or antichristianism is around them; and what the chill of that is, one must feel to know. Their temptations are perhaps greater than those of ordinary Christians, and their external aids certainly less. It is well to realize these truths, that we may turn them into prayers.

The way in which the Bible is recalled to one at every moment is wonderful. It seems as if Oriental life had been petrified into immutability to prove for ever the marvellous minute truthfulness of Scriptural narrative. At Pompeii you have the scenery of ancient life restored; in the East, in many respects, you have the life itself,—

that is, in all of the East that lies below the thin gilding of poor French civilization at the upper surface.

Yesterday we rested and enjoyed some bread and water under the shade of a twin palm. At first the palm-trees do not give you hope of much shade, but at noon you feel the beautiful crown, with its leaves folding thickly over each other, shelter you from the vertical sun like an impenetrable green umbrella, whilst the waving of the deeply cut leaves in the breeze far above cools you like a fan, and sounds like a cascade of water. It is worth while to have experienced this heat, to learn what the Bible means by shade. The burning sand of the desert on the edge of which the Pyramids stand heats the air several feet high; the glow from the sun and the sand above and beneath meet, and you can imagine under these circumstances what a boon the shade of a cloud, or a palm-tree, or a great rock, or even a block of stone must be.

We begin to understand the people "riding on asses;" burdens being carried here on asses and camels, and all classes riding on them, horses being only used for war or great pomp.

Then the flocks of sheep and goats feeding together; the "swift dromedaries" accompanying the pasha's cavalry; the deep wells, by the side of which, if you had "nothing to draw with," you might die of thirst; the prostrations in prayer; the throwing off of the outer garment, or girding it up; the veil with which the women cover themseves;—it makes so many old words become *things!* And all the prophecies about Egypt, and the little incidental allusions to peculiar Egyptian scenery and customs, which one had scarcely noticed, one at once feels their truthfulness here, so that Exodus seems fresh, like a book written yesterday. The way in which "the river" is constantly mentioned is so characteristically Egyptian, —*e. g.*, "Pharaoh's daughter coming to bathe in the river," and Pharaoh coming to "the river." The Nile is so completely the centre of Egyptian life; agriculture, commerce, all depend on it. The river is the bath, drinking-fountain, rain-cloud, soil and manure-factory, and high-road of the whole country; their seasons are divided by it; their chronology dates from its inundations. Egypt altogether is such a peculiar land, that one may well be thankful the Bible was not written by men who lived in it, or its imagery would have been incomprehensible to all the world beside. Instead of this God committed the writing of his word to a people dwelling in a land possessing (as Mr. Stanley says), more variety of climate and scenery than any other in the world; so that mountaineers, mariners, shepherds, citizens, husbandmen, all find their mode of life reflected in its pages. What can one say of the condescending care for our tastes and ways which such a fact implies, but, like the negro, when asked if he did not wonder at the love shown by the Lord Jesus in suffering for us, "No, massa, me no wonder, it be so *like* Him."....

Monday.—After our return from the Shoubra gardens, we rode to Mr. Lieder's, and on our way had to keep close by the side of the narrow streets to let a Coptic funeral pass. We first heard a series of wild, loud, unearthly shrieks, and then six women mounted on donkeys rode rapidly by us, wailing as they went, folded from head to foot in black silk. One beat on a tambourine, the others wailed that strange prolonged cry like the yell of despair or madness, or a long hopeless shriek of pain, yet fearfully measured and regular, as the beat of the waves against a wreck. Then there came the bier, carried rapidly above the bearers' heads, covered with a pink pall. "Without hope in the world" seemed to ring terribly through that strange cry, mechanical as of course it was. There was nothing of appeal or entreaty about it; it seemed like a frantic struggle against an irresistible impersonal fate. We thought of the minstrels and people making a noise, and the theatrical wailing which could so lightly turn into scornful laughter at the Deliverer. With what meaning it brought to our hearts the apostle's words, "Sorrow not as others, who have no hope!"

Tuesday.—This morning we started on our final donkey-ride to see old Cairo. On reaching it, we threaded our way (after a beautiful breezy country ride), through narrow alleys and passages under the stone arch of the old Roman Prætorium, up stone staircases which Antony and Cleopatra may have ascended. Antony and Cleopatra seem almost our cotemporaries in this land, whose history counts by millenniums. Above these staircases, at the end of broad stone corridors, we found two Coptic churches, and one Greek church, perched like eagles' nests high up in the old palace of the Roman governors of the Egyptian Babylon. The Coptic church contains no images, but pictures like the Greek. They are divided into four parts. The sanctuary, which the priests alone may enter, is separated from the rest of the church by a high solid screen of wood. On this, the barrier which excludes the people from the holy place, the art and money of the builders seems to have been lavished. The material of those we saw was ebony, overlaid with ivory, and most elaborately carved. These screens are strangely typical. It is the old system; all man's ingenuity spent in reconstructing and decorating the veil which God's hand has rent for ever from top to bottom. In this the corrupt churches of the West trace their own lineaments. The stream was tainted before it divided. But in one point we noticed a difference between the superstitions of the East and the West. Our guide explained a sculpture which we remarked, to mean a group of angels, to whom he gave various cabalistic sounding names. He was evidently wrong: it was a carving of the twelve apostles, but the direction in which his thoughts ran struck us. In the West it would have been, not angels, but saints; and the contrast led the mind back to the wild Oriental Gnostic heresies which ad their origin in this very region.

In quitting Cairo for Alexandria, you leave the strange unchanging East, and the vast, silent, ancient world, and enter a bustling commercial seaport. Once an exchange for thought, it is now merely a mart for things. The mysterious, solitary, single-blocked pillar called Pompey's, and the widowed obelisk called Cleopatra's, stand on heaps of sand and rubbish quite outside the motley modern seaport, more desolate than if they stood alone in the sand wastes. Silent deserts of time stretch between them and the poor buildings close to them. They stand monuments, not merely of a city, but of civilizations and races passed away. Cæsar's Camp in the solitudes, some miles away, seemed far less lonely; and it was strange to walk quietly by the sea-shore on which it stands, and pick up the shells and watch the waves —the same little shells one gathers in England, and waves with the same music we listened to as children on the coast of Cornwall, strange to feel how nature and human life flow ever the same and ever new, beneath and above all the changes of national history.

III.

On the Mediterranean.

JOPPA—RAMLEH—JERUSALEM.

SUNDAYS are delightful days in travelling. The bodily rest; the repose to eye and ear from the duty of seeing and hearing as much as possible; the pause to meditate on the past; the thoughts of home and all familiar things, the thoughts of heaven and the Father in heaven as near us as those at home; the certainty that on this day at least our hearts are travelling the same road, however far apart our steps may be—all these things make Sunday especially precious to the traveller.

In this little French steamer, in itself any thing but comfortable, we have one great luxury—there are no ladies on board, so we have the ladies' cabin to ourselves. As it was too hot to attempt the desert journey, we find some especial pleasures in this little interval on the sea. It is very strange to have the history and geography which have become allegories to us, translated again into everyday facts, and to be actually "from Egypt lately come," on our way between Egypt and Canaan, pilgrims to the Holy City.

Our little ship is an epitome of the visible Church, or rather of the world; and to those on board, the literal Egypt and Canaan bring associations as different as the spiritual Egypt and Canaan would. There are Egyptians, Jews, Turks, Greeks, Armenians, a Sister of Charity, and a pious Protestant Frenchman.

The sweep of the two harbors at Alexandria looked very fine as we left. In fancy we rebuilt the temples, palaces, and forts, on the sandy mounds which stretch on each side of the modern city, with its minarets, Pompey's Pillar, and the white palace of the Pacha gleaming from far over the blue sea.

At the hotel we met a strange waif of the

European world, a German waiter, who had traveled as one of a wanderng band of musicians, through Russia, Austria, Italy, and Syria. With some difficulty we procured a German Testament and gave it him. His delight and gratitude were very great.

To-day, as we were reading our Bibles on deck, a French fellow-voyager observed it, and remarked how happy it was to travel with those of one mind. He had been trying to speak of Christ to some Arabs on board. We gave him some of our Italian and Greek tracts to distribute among the deck passengers. He came back with a beaming face. "Ils étaient si contents," they were "thirsting for more." We gladly supplied him. We feel it such a blessed touch, as it were, of the hand of God, being given these little services to do.

The French Sister of Charity on board has a sensible, benevolent face. She has been telling me of their Orphan Asylum and Hospital at Alexandria, and of the Sisters of St. Joseph at Jaffa and Jerusalem. I said it was sweet to think that whatever was done for the poor, thinking of our Lord and for his sake, he looked on as done unto him. She seemed to feel it. I think with Roman Catholics the best way is to point to that central truth of our religion, which, in words at least, we hold in common. If once the heart really reaches that central point, the person and redeeming death of the Son of God, all the fabric of error will either crumble into dust, or at least lose its power to hide from the light which is life.

JOPPA.

At sunset we caught our first glimpse of the Holy Land, from the *passerelle* of the French steamer. We stood there half an hour gazing at it. The undulating coast grew clearer as we looked; the white houses of Joppa rose one above the other on the steep hill side; two other villages stood out more clearly in the reflected glow of the sunset; and behind them stretched the range of hills which divides the plain of the coast from Jerusalem. In the west the sun was setting, tinging with rose and gold the first rain clouds we had seen since we reached Egypt. The sun of the Holy Land has gone westward, but it will return to the east.

It was too late to disembark that evening, but we landed early on Tuesday morning. And now we are actually standing on the Holy Land. It certainly wonderfully brings home the humanity of our Lord, to see the very country where he dwelt and went about doing good.

RAMLEH.

At Jaffa we found a clean, cool hotel, kept by a German Jew. Inserted into the lintel of one of the doors was a little glass cylinder, enclosing a parchment roll, on which was left visible, in Hebrew, the name of God revealed to Abraham (Shaddai),—the Almighty, the All-sufficient. We remarked it to the host, and he said it was a Jewish custom to remind those who entered the house of the presence of God. They had placed it, he said, on the lintel of every door; but Frenchmen, who did not read the Bible, sometimes mocked at it, and this led to angry discussion, so that from many of the doors it was now removed. Protestants understood it because they read the Bible.

The inn was the first specimen of an Oriental house—not a palace or a hotel in the French style—which we had entered. The entrance was by a narrow flight of stone steps into a court-yard, then up another flight of exterior stone steps to a platform, which was the roof of one room and the entrance to two others.

The view from one of the windows of the house-tops of Jaffa was interesting. On some of these, beds (that is, rugs) were spread; on others, earthen pitchers, or vegetables and fruit were lying. Every house has thus several house tops. Before breakfast we read all we could find in the Bible about Joppa and the neighboring coast, the Book of Jonah, and the stories of Cornelius and Dorcas. We thought of the Church once existing there, the six brethren who accompanied St. Peter thence along the rich plain and the undulating coast to Cæsarea, and of the trance at mid-day on one of the many house-tops such as those around us.

We breakfasted in a pleasant, open alcove, looking on the sea. It was interesting to enter the little haven of Jaffa, which is guarded from the storms of the open Mediterranean by a singular and natural breakwater, a semi-circular reef of rocks, and think that Jonah must have fled through the same entrance. The little haven was as smooth as a lake when we were there, in contrast with the waves breaking outside. Only small craft can enter; an English frigate lay outside, but many fishing-boats and small fruit vessels were moored inside. I found the children of the house knew the history of Jonah. "It is in the old Bible," they said in German. I spoke to the Jewish host about the land having been once their own, and the prophecy that it should be once more their own, when they acknowledged Jesus as the Christ. He said, Yes, he had heard that some Christians believed their land would be restored to them when they acknowledged Him who died 1800 years ago at Jerusalem as their Messiah.

We walked to "Simon the tanner's house." In this house is an ancient well, with a deep groove worn in its stone edge by the rope which draws up the bucket. The water was quite sweet. From the house-top we looked over a sandy beach to the sea It was on *such* a house-top that Peter saw the vision which showed him the wall of partition between Jew and Gentile broken down for ever, by the same atoning sacrifice which rent the veil between man and God; on such a house-top, and on this very scene he looked, before the glorious vision veiled earth and sea from his entranced eyes.

This is the true, undying interest of travelling in the Holy Land—it is not whether or not we enter the material houses, or tread on the identical clods which apostles touched or trod on, but in this unchanging East—it was *such* a house as this, such a house-top, and a surrounding scene of plain, and sea, and rock, the very same. On this very identical little glassy haven St. Peter looked; along this very coast the messengers from Cornelius came and went; through that one widest break in the rocky breakwater Jonah fled. Our bodies may not, cannot touch the identical particles of earth, but our eyes and minds do indeed gaze on the identical scenes.

We went through the bazaar to a Saracenic fountain, just outside the town, and tried to sketch the picturesque groups collected there—Bedouins in grand historical attitudes with spears and striped bornouses; children in quaint repetitions of the costumes of their elders, with bright dark eyes and red fezes; and white-veiled women. A white horse stooped to drink at the fountain or trough, files of camels and donkeys were led there, and slaves came and filled their graceful brown pitchers. The other point of view from which we attempted a sketch was on the sea-shore. On one side rose the old fortified town above the smooth little haven, girded with rocks and breakers, and filled with small vessels, their rigging quaintly curved as in old pictures. On the other side we looked across the gardens and orchards of pears, oranges and peaches, hedged with prickly pear, to the hill country of Judea.

The town must be much the same as in the oldest times. The form of the ground fixes the line of the street; and up and down and round and round, at sharp angles and in sudden curves, they wind and turn, often with vaulted roofs which form the ground of the street above,—cool, narrow streets, half arched over, presenting windows and wooden lattices richly carved, sometimes a fragment of a prostrate marble column forming a door step, and all brilliant as an illuminated Missal with the deep and varied coloring of Oriental costume.

We had difficulty in procuring horses, and

then quite a melodramatic skirmish with the owners of the wretched animals we had hired, because they wanted not only the earnest money which we had paid, but the whole sum before we started. They clung to the manes and tails of the horses, and made a great storm in the market place ; but it seemed merely a theatrical display, subsiding instantaneously when we finally broke from them and they saw we were determined not to yield.

We rode for a mile or two through beautiful fruit gardens, orange, peach, &c., bordered with impenetrable hedges of prickly pear, and then across a wide flat of recently reaped fields of corn, occasionally varied by an ancient grove of grey olives, or a patch of maize or tobacco, and a few solitary palms, not like the palm forests of Egypt, but scattered singly here and there. Once or twice we passed a drove of camels, or a herd of sheep and goats, and a few cows watched by Arab herd boys. All the afternoon the hills of Judea were full in view, a series of hills rising one out of another with little variety of outline, but beautiful to our eyes after the levels of Egypt, and at sunset bathed in the loveliest rose and violet. And this was the plain of Sharon, and beyond those hills lay Jerusalem! As I rode it was a great joy to look round on this land where our Saviour did indeed walk patiently about doing good, and was so often wearied at noon by the burden and heat of the day.

Quærens me sedisti lassus
Redemisti crucem passus,
Tantus labor non sit cassus.

Weary sat'st Thou, seeking me,
Diedst redeeming on the tree,
Not in vain such toil can be!

JERUSALEM.

We started at six o'clock in the morning from Ramleh, packing hard eggs, salt, oranges, and bread into our bag as provision for the long day's journey, there being not a house where refreshment could be procured on all the way to Jerusalem. All of our horses were worn-out and slow, or disabled in some way, so that we could not get beyond a walk or a jog-trot. After leaving Ramleh, with its minarets and rambling houses, we rode through a few fruit gardens like those near Jaffa, and after these through bare, brown stubble fields where the harvest had just been gathered in. Gradually the country became more stony and undulating till we were quite among the hills. At first we rode through a range of low hills, like a burnt-up Dartmoor, without grass, or heather, or furz; then, as we penetrated further into the country the hills became higher and the valleys deeper, and green shrubs in many places covered the hollows where in winter the torrents flow. The road lay along the beds of dry torrents, over smooth slabs of rocks on the hill-sides, and amongst thick beds of water-worn stones in the valleys, up and down flights of rock stairs, over which the water must rush in cascades in the rainy season.

The dip of the strata is strangely perceptible on those bare hills. Ranges of natural rock terraces, at a distance, reminding us of the terraced vine hills of the Côte d'Or, only without the vines,—the forms round and monotonous. In some of the valleys we passed groves of old olives, and wild fig-trees grew here and there on the hillocks. Half-way between Jaffa and Jerusalem we came to a ruined building, a chapel. Olives were springing out of its crevices and growing around, and some Arabs were resting in the shade. We hoped to have found water here; the horses had been watered an hour before, drinking eagerly out of a round cavity in a stone filled from a pit close by. But after dismounting and resting a few minutes, we discovered there was no spring or cistern near, and as no time was to be lost, we rode on at once.

Half an hour's more climbing brought us to an upland valley, where there was an ancient grove of olives; and here we halted for our mid-day rest, and disposed of our oranges and eggs, and most thankfully received some water which a peasant brought in a skin from a rain-tank a little distance off. It was delicious to rest against the trunk of an old olive, looking up to the pure sky through the silver leaves, and feeling the breeze.

After we left our noonday resting-place, the interest of our journey deepened. We began to look forward to Jerusalem. From the first height beyond our halting-place we looked back over the labyrinth of hills we had been threading to the plain of Ramleh; then the Mediterranean came in sight. After that our thoughts turned steadfastly forward towards Jerusalem, and the anxiety to catch the first glimpse became intense. Every ridge we mounted we hoped to see it, and as one hill, with its rock terraces folded over another, we fancied every fold we turned would reveal it; but four hours more remained of weary clambering up and down the rocky mountain paths. We passed a large village, with old ruinous buildings; then we came to a delicious spring of cool, pure water, and drank rock-water for the first time for weeks, out of the spout of an earthen pitcher, and thought of the "cup of cold water." Beyond this another village appeared on the summit of a hill, with white walls, domes, and minarets. Some of us thought this must be a suburb of Jerusalem, but we were soon undeceived. About this time we met some Syrian peasants, but could not make them understand us; until just as we thought Jerusalem *must* be almost in sight, another Arab met us, and in answer to our eager inquiries, counted on his fingers "an hour and a half."

Our spirits sank, the road became still rougher, in some places dangerously steep and rugged, so that some of our party dismounted; it was, indeed, like riding over a dry waterfall, the stones polished by water in winter, and pilgrims in summer, whilst our poor horses became more and more tired and stumbled from fatigue. At length we reached a stony ridge beyond which no height seemed to rise. Yet there was no glimpse of Jerusalem to greet our weary eyes; still on and on over the loose stones and slabs of rock on that level mountain ridge, until we almost despaired of reaching the city before sunset closed the gates; and then, suddenly, *it was there!* Across a slight depression in the high table-land rose dome, and minaret, and the long western wall!

In a few minutes we reached the Jaffa Gate. We were in time; the gates were not yet closed. The feeling of being actually *there* was overpowering beyond anything I had imagined of it. Old familiar Bible words and sentences rushed into the mind, and especially the verse, "Our feet shall stand in thy gates, O Jerusalem."

I was glad that a little stumbling and kicking among the horses diverted the overwhelming rush of emotions, until we reached our cool room in Simeon Rosenthal's hotel on

Mount Zion. There I could enjoy a satisfactory solitary burst of irrepressible tears, while those words came into my heart in the way in which Bible words do come to us at some rare moments, as if spoken in the heart by a voice which is not that of our own thoughts—not ours, and yet within our inmost soul, "*Come unto me, all ye that are weary and heavy-laden, and I will give you rest.*" In that very city, almost within hearing of where I was resting then, those Divine words had indeed sounded in a human voice—how divine, and how human! It was as if body and spirit were steeped for a time in a rapture of perfect rest.

After a short repose and dinner, I went to be quiet again in our room, but heard voices on the roof, and mounted there. Our hotel is on one of the highest points of Mount Zion. On the east the Mount of Olives rose beyond the platform of the Temple, with its three brown summits and its small mosque. The valley of the Kedron, which divides Olivet from the Temple, was quite hidden from us, and in the clear atmosphere it was difficult to realize there was any valley between. From the "Castle of David" on the west waved the flag of the Crescent; from the minaret on the north near the Church of the Holy Sepulchre the muezzin shouted his truth and his lie. Forty or fifty feet below this miserable Turkish town, with its domes and minarets, lay the site of the City of God, the Holy City, which nevertheless spiritually is called Sodom and Egypt, where also our Lord was crucified. All is deserted, accursed, desolated, worse than a solitude, "trodden under foot of the Gentiles;" yet here His voice was heard! In those temple-precincts which stretch beneath us sounded the "woes" which hypocrite and oppressor stood entranced in their own despite to hear; and there the blind and lame came to him and He healed them. A human voice which would not have reached as far as where I stood; but words how divine!

IV.

Jerusalem

AND ITS NEIGHBORHOOD.

MOUNT ZION, *Thursday.*

YOU would wonder at my finding any time to write, if you saw our expeditions. Our walks are all scrambles, and our rides steeple-chases, so that every excursion involves repairs to a great extent. Then there are sketches to be made, and thus every moment is brimful of business.

Jerusalem strikes us as a more complete desolation than Memphis or Heliopolis—"trodden under foot"—the present wretched town built far above the ruins of the old, on heaps of rubbish. They had to dig fifty feet for the foundations of the English church on Zion, so that the slightest risings and hollows which determined the direction of streets in the ancient city must in a great degree be lost. The delight is to leave the city and wander about these valleys, gaze on the hills, and tread the very slopes, and even the very roads and paths, which the feet of our Saviour trod. It certainly does wonderfully help one to realize his humanity. Especially the paths interest us. In all countries, antiquaries say, nothing changes less than footpaths; the church paths often remaining unchanged from century to century, leading successive generations of peasants, perhaps, to successive generations of churches. The ways traced out almost unconsciously by the feet of men outlive the laborious erections of their hands; and if this is true in busy, restless, populous England, in Palestine it is emphatically the case. No new roads have been made here since the days of the Romans, probably no new sites fixed on since the days of the Canaanites. The merchant carrying wares from Damascus to Sidon probably drives his mules along the same paths as Hiram's or Solomon's. The peasant bringing vegetables from Bethany to Jerusalem treads the same paths as Lazarus trod, and Mary and Martha. The rain torrents are the only road makers, and any changes that have been effected on the roads must be attributed to them. And when we consider how our Lord patiently sought out and visited every city and village, this fact of the enduring nature of mountain paths brings his life home to us often with a vividness which is startling. Almost one can fancy one catches the wave of a garment through those olives, or the glimpse of a dim, retreating form disappearing over that hill-top, of the little band that went about with him. And then we cast aside fancy altogether, as an unworthy denizen of this land of glorious and terrible truths, and remember, "*He was here.*" Scene after scene of these wondrous narratives as minute as any fiction, and more truthful than any other history, rises unbidden to the memory, and the silent hills are musical with words which shall outlive them by an eternity.

The sweep of the hill of Zion, from its summit above Moriah to the depths of the craggy Valley of Hinmon, is very fine. Every where the rocks are excavated into tombs, mostly very ancient. Wherever water is, there is luxuriant green. Only cultivation is wanted to transform these brown hills of rock and dry clods into slopes and terraces rich with every kind of vegetation. Terraces to bank up the earth are needed, and reservoirs to store the water which now lays waste the land by its overflow at one season, and leaves it parched by drought at another. Palestine—at least this part of it—never could have been a country which would be fertile without cultivation; but, with it, it produces any thing in the richest abundance.

This morning we went with Miss Creasy. who kindly called for us, to see Miss Cooper's industrial school.* We went by the Via

* This was in 1856. How solemn the lapse of a few years often makes the most trivial entries in a diary. Since then Miss Creasy has been murdered just outside

Dolorosa, and glanced into the church of the Holy Sepulchre ; surely *not* the street He trod, *not* Calvary.

The school interested us deeply. The Jewish women sat on divans around the walls of the various rooms, busily engaged in sewing, knitting, &c. Miss Creasy told us Miss Cooper's Jewesses were known throughout Jerusalem by their superior neatness. Every day a chapter in the Old Testament is read to them, about which they are questioned, and a chapter in the New Testament, about which they cannot be questioned. The rabbis have more than once denounced and scattered the school, but after a time it has quietly gathered again. The prejudices of the women are apparently not shaken. They would not drink a draught of water except out of cups especially reserved for their use, and kept

---

the walls of Jerusalem, Miss Cooper, after a brief visit to England, returned to die at the post she had so devotedly held for so many years, and Mr. Nicolayson also is gone. The Bishop was absent during our visit.

from the pollution of Gentile lips ; and even from those cups which are kindly set apart for them they will often only drink through their veils, as an additional safeguard. Miss Cooper did not speak of any direct instances of spiritual good, but I was much struck with her reply when I tried to comfort her for this by saying the seed sown in faith could not be without blessed result. "I am *sure* of it," she said very quietly, but with a hope that was evidently firm as a possession. She believed her Master had called her to this work —she had obeyed his call ; and if to her dying day she saw not a result, she was content to wait. He had sent ner, and her labor could not be in vain, whatever were its results.

This afternoon we had a long ride round by the north side of the city, over the Mount of Olives to Bethany, and home (home to Jerusalem !) by another road over the brook Kedron. Mr. Nicolayson kindly undertook to be our guide. The day before I had been twelve hours in the saddle, and to-day I had a bad saddle, which kept turning round. We were a large party, some officers of a frigate off Jaffa having joined us. Every one was so kind in helping me through my difficulties; but my horse was very slow, and I could not bear to keep others back, and when I came home I could not help feeling exceedingly vexed to think how fatigue and discomfort had occupied my mind on my first introduction to scenes of such intense interest. It was very humbling, and perhaps taught me as much as if all earthly things had been swallowed up, (as under other circumstances they might) in the sacred recollections of the places.

Mr. Nicolayson particularly directed our attention to the view from the north side of Olivet; the city lying in the bosom of the hills, the high table land on the edge of which it stands, backed by the distant "hill country of Judea." This, he thought, explained the meaning of the verse, "Beautiful for situation, the joy of the whole earth, is Mount Sion, on [or from] the sides of the north, the city of the great King." A plantation of mulberries beyond the Jaffa Gate, belonging to the Greek convent, showed what the country might be made with cultivation. On the opposite side we saw the blue mirror of the Dead Sea, with the Jordan flowing into it, and the Perean hills beyond, a scene of the wildest desolation. We came home by the wretched little mountain hamlet of Bethany, with its cabins built of rough stones, and its unhomelike flat roofs. In the hill side we dismounted at a cave which is called the grave of Lazarus, and such a cave in this very place it certainly was. From the village we rode up the high road from Jericho. There stood on a height the remains of another flat roofed village over against you, and about this point we caught a glimpse of the tops of the houses of Jerusalem, but lost sight of them again in a winding descent of one of the intervening heights; and then, when we reached this second height, the whole city burst on our sight, across the Valley of Jehoshaphat, sloping upwards from the edge of the steep of Moriah,—the Temple platform, flat roofed houses, and the Castle of David on the height of Zion, rising before us as distinct as the successive seats in a Roman amphitheatre. It is this first glimpse of the roofs of the city, then lost again, and succeeded by the sudden bursting of the whole on your sight, which is suggested in "Stanley's Palestine," as explaining the repetition of the words, "and when he was come nigh," in St. Luke's narrative. At the first indication that they were approaching the city (Luke xix. 37,) "the whole multitude of the disciples began to rejoice and praise God with a loud voice." Then when the whole guilty city suddenly spread itself before the Saviour's eyes from that second height,—the Temple where he had warned, and pleaded, and healed,—the Golgotha outside the walls, where he was to die, "he beheld the city and wept over it." We re-entered Jerusalem by the Jaffa Gate. The evening we spent at the English consul's. The pasha was there, and we had some conversation with him through an interpreter.

Friday.

We went in the morning with a guide from our hotel through what are popularly called "The Tombs of the Kings." They are catacombs, honeycombing the earth outside the city. We entered two or three, creeping through low, narrow rock passages into a large chamber surrounded with ledges cut in the rocky sides, and frequently leading by stone doors into other chambers similarly ledged. These ledges were too narrow for stone sarcophagi, or even for coffins; they seemed only fit for bodies "wrapped in a linen cloth," and embalmed "as the manner of the Jews is to bury." All the entrances had been closed with stone—some with carved stone doors, turning on stone hinges—some apparently with a large unhewn stone, which "covered the mouth." These little coincidences with the New Testament narratives are very interesting as circumstantial evidence, and delightful in enabling us to bring home the old familiar gospel stories. They make one feel as if it might all have happened yesterday. Outside one of the more modern tombs was a carved stone sarcophagus, and in another one or two sarcophagi, too small for any but a child.

In the afternoon, at the commencement of the Jews' Sabbath, we went to their wailing place, where some large ancient stones still mark the old walls of the Temple precincts. A narrow lane divides this wall from some high buildings opposite, and against these several men sat on the ground intoning Hebrew psalms. Two white-veiled women stood and pressed their faces against the stones, weeping and wailing, so that their whole frames quivered with sobs. How much of this is dramatic or ceremonial, I do not know. But it was an affecting scene, not so much from the thought of what they *felt*, as of what they *are*, in comparison with what they might have been—outcast, despised and degraded, having exchanged the joyous music of their sanctuary for vain wailings by the outer wall, which, at peril of life, they dare not pass.

Leaving that strangely typical company, we scrambled through a garden and a hedge of prickly pear, into a field close to another portion of the old wall of Moriah. Here some of the lower stones are twenty feet in length, and with a graving at the edge, which is said to be Jewish or Phœnician,—the very stones, perhaps, which were hewn in the distant Tyrian quarries, and then silently fitted into their places in the Temple, types of the living stones quarried and chiselled on earth, with many a blow, for their places in heaven. Above them is the spring of the first arch of the bridge by which Herod connected Moriah with his palace on Zion, and above the smaller stones of the Saracenic wall, looking like children's work in contrast with the massive masonry of earlier times. As you look from this point away from the Temple area, the Mount of Olives rises before you, with one palm-tree in the distance, relic of the grove which supplied the palm-branches to strew the way for our Lord's triumphal entry—the one poor visible triumph of his life on earth, made sweet by children's voices.

We finished our expedition by visits to two Jewish families. The head of the first was a fine patriarchal looking old man with two wives, the younger quite young and pretty, with three beautiful dark eyed children. The inner room was a divan, with a view over the temple court to the Mount of Olives. The second family were Karaite Jews from Russia, who reject the Talmud, founding their faith on the Old Testament only. They were very courteous. The courtyards, as we entered, were exceedingly dirty, but the houses themselves seemed cool and comparatively clean, many of the rooms having those airy domed roofs which give such picturesqueness to the towns of Southern Syria.

Saturday.

This has been a high day indeed. The Temple area, the precincts of the "Mosque of the Dome of the Rock,"* the Haram, more sacred to Moslems than any spot on earth except Mecca, fiercely contended for during mediæval centuries, and jealously guarded from every infidel foot for centuries since, is this year opened to European parties by the pasha of Jerusalem "for a consideration," and to-day we went over it! When this was first attempted, the Pasha invited the fanatical mollahs to breakfast, and politely detained them until the infidels were safely out of the Haram. To enter a corner of the precincts even now, except on these occasions, would be to peril life, but we were secured by a Turkish guard. With the accompaniments of Turkish guards and guides, thought and feeling were of course benumbed. All we could do was to turn ourselves as far as possible into eye and ear, and treasure up stores for memory.

The precincts are very large, surrounded

---

* Commonly, but, we were told, incorrectly, called the Mosque of Omar.

with cloisters and high walls, towards the city; in the steeper part of the Kedron and Hinnom valleys, the walls meet the rock and form a strong fortification, especially at the angle of the valleys of Kedron and Hinnom. The larger part of this platform is not covered with masonry, but is a clear space, sprinkled with pomegranates and cypresses, with here and there a shrine, and one arched well, from which pure living water is drawn in buckets. We gathered some leaves and little flowers here. Above this space rises the platform of the great mosque, paved with marble, and ascended by a flight of white marble steps, surmounted by a beautifully carved screen or open gateway, also of white marble. It is the contrast of this with the fine dark cypresses which is so striking from the Mount of Olives, and recalls Josephus's description of Herod's temple, "a mountain of snow tipped with gold." The mosque is very beautiful, with a kind of barbaric Moorish beauty. The octagonal walls below the dome are covered with porcelain mosaic, the roof inside is of the richest woods, inlaid and carved, the floors of marble mosaic, the windows like jewellery of small pieces of brilliant Venetian stained glass. Beautiful columns, and an elaborately worked balustrade, surround the Holy Stone, which Moslems believe to be the centre of the world, suspended from heaven by an invisible golden chain. It is a huge projection of the native rock of Moriah, the sloping summit, indeed, or peak of the hill, and must evidently have been spared for some special purpose to break through the usual level to which the Temple area was reduced. Some think it was the threshing-floor of Araunah the Jebusite, since large slabs of rock are constantly used for that purpose in the mountain villages of this sunny land. Underneath it is a cavern, which is a Moslem sanctuary, containing four exquisitely carved marble shrines (apparently taken from the earlier Christian churches of

Helena or Justinian), and called respectively the praying-places of Abraham, David, Solomon, and St. George. It was strange to encounter our old friend of the dragon-conflict in such society, but Moslem traditions are happily so entirely independent of facts, as in no way to perplex the historian. A plastered wall conceals the end of this cavern, so as not to belie the Moslem theory of the miraculous suspension of the rock between earth and heaven. In the floor of the cave is inserted a circular marble stone, which gives a hollow sound when you strike it. It is the mouth of a deep pit, by which it is believed the living may have access to the souls of the departed, but the attempt of some bereaved ones to obtain such intercourse led to madness, and it is not now permitted. Oh, yearning human heart, beneath all the follies and hypocrisies of dead or false creeds, how alike it beats! And here, *here* the Voice once was heard which pierced through all its disguises, and met all its yearnings, and brought the longed-for tidings from that other world: the Voice we know, for it speaks to us still.

What were this cavern and this mysterious pit? Were they connected with the Temple sacrifices? Did the blood of the sacrifices flow here, protesting for centuries that without shedding of blood is no remission, until the true sacrifice was offered in no sacred place, but on a Golgotha, and the full propitiation was made which renders every place on earth as sacred as this was once? Were we, indeed, treading that sacred spot which for centuries no mortal foot trod save that of the high priests once every year? Roman fires and ploughshares, and heathen rites and Moslem ignorance have blotted out the answer. Here, as elsewhere in the Holy Land, our interest is in the general scenery, and not in any sacred spot of earth, as best befits a religion founded on facts, which, while it rejects the sentimentalism of sacred places, welcomes the confirmation of geography and history.

We descended the marble steps again,

looked back through the arched screen on the beautiful great mosque, and crossed the green space to the beautiful Mosque El Aska, formerly the church of Justinian. It is a Greek church, Mohammedanized by the abstraction of all the pictures and Christian symbols, by praying mats directed towards Mecca, and by gigantic Arabic inscriptions from the Koran on the columns. Near what was once the high altar, was a small marble canopy enshrining (the Moslems say) "an impression of the foot of Jesus." There is a third mosque on the Temple area, smaller than the others, and very plain. This is the original Mosque of Omar. It has windows looking across the Valley of the Kedron, very steep at this point.

The whole of the area is excavated underneath into arched vaults, supported by massive columns. We looked down through a crevice into this. There are also enormous water tanks below.

After visiting the little simple Mosque of Omar, we descended by a marble flight of steps to the vault underneath the Mosque El Aska, leading to the Golden Gate in the wall above the Kedron valley, which the Moslems have walled up and jealously guard to prevent "*Him whom the Jews expect*" from "fulfilling the old prophecy, and entering Jerusalem." A long, broad flight of worn and broken steps leads to this gate, which must have been one of the ancient entrances. Near it are columns of gigantic size, I think with lotus capitals, like some of those in Egyptian temples. Among them was one with a Corinthian capital. The walls were built of large blocks of stone.

When we left this mysterious vault or crypt, we mounted the wall of the Temple area near it, and sat there quietly some little time. On the outside of the wall close to us was inserted a fragment of an ancient column projecting over the Valley of Jehoshaphat, on which, according to Moslem tradition, Mohammed is to sit to judge the world. All around, the rocky sides of the valleys are perforated with tombs, ancient and modern, for here the Jews also expect to stand before the Judge. And on that brown hill opposite it is written, "His feet shall stand, and it shall cleave in the midst thereof toward the east and toward the west, and there shall be a very great valley, and the Lord my God shall come, and all the saints with thee."

Turning towards the city, the Temple area lay spread before us. There, on that hill, Abraham's heart rejoiced when the trial of his faith was over, and the ram was substituted for his Isaac; there David gazed and longed to build the Temple, and when forbidden the higher work, with a noble submission and self-sacrifice accepted the lower, and prepared the stones; there, at length, (on whatever exact spot, whether on the site of either of the mosques or between them), *there* the glorious Temple stood—the hills rung with the joyous music of the great dedication feast; there the divine ceremonial was carried on; and there, at last, Jesus sat and taught, and denounced the hypocrites, and healed the lame and the blind, and stood and cried, "If any man thirst, let him come unto me and drink," greater than Solomon, greater than the Temple—" my Lord and my God."

All this and much much more seemed to rush through the mind in those few minutes, as we sat on the temple wall—somewhat in the way in which they say the whole of a past life rises before the drowning man—and then we rejoined the party, and left the sacred courts.

The pasha entertained us with coffee and chibouques as we went away.

The afternoon was to me even more interesting, because we were left to ourselves, and escaped from the degraded city into the valleys around. We had a delightful quiet walk, out at the Zion Gate, through fields of rough parched clods. Thorns, long as little daggers, strong and sharp, grew on many of the bushes, and reminded us of the crown once plaited from them. Pomegranates were scattered here and there, their rich scarlet blossoms shining through the fresh green of their foliage. We passed several rock cave-tombs excavated in the hills, on our way to what is called the Pool of Siloam. It is a large tank or reservoir hewn in the rock, and completed with masonry. It contained a little muddy water when we were there. Above it, at the upper end, was a rock terrace, from which a rough arched door-way led down a flight of rock steps to a cavern over a stream of sweet living water. We descended to it and watched it flowing underneath the hill, until the ripple was lost in the subterranean darkness. This stream finds its way underneath the rock terrace to the "Pool of Siloam." Its source is a mystery; we found it again higher up. Bases of broken columns rise on one side of this tank. At the lower end a narrow stone stair leads to the water which flows out from it to some troughs for watering the flocks and herds, a little further down the valley. These at four o'clock in the afternoon we found nearly empty. One of our party had seen them full in the morning.

The water is turned off, after the cattle are watered in the morning, to irrigate some gardens lower down the valley. This is the pleasantest, greenest place we have seen near Jerusalem. There was the delicious sound of abundant water falling, and pomegranates, mulberries, and figs in their freshest green. Thence we walked by the gnarled old tree, where tradition says Isaiah was sawn asunder, to another tank with a little stagnant green water or mud at the bottom of it, and close to it was a rude building, covering a fine deep well. Water was drawn up from it for us by a long rope, and we drank it from a skin. It was sweet.

We returned through the village of Siloam, with its flat-roofed stone cabins and small cisterns or rain-tanks cut in the rock before every door. Leaving the village, we came to the Fountain of the Virgin, a cavern in the hill-side underneath the city. We descended by a broad flight of stone built steps, and then by a narrow, rock-hewn stair, and drank of the sweet crystal water.

It was the same as that we had tasted before in the stream which feeds Siloam. But it is not the spring. Again, as we tried to trace it, its flow was lost in darkness. It is said either to flow from a spring of living water which rises underneath the Temple, or to be supplied from Solomon's aqueducts from the south. We passed by a "place of skulls," or at least of graves and bones—a spur of Moriah, overlooking quiet retreats of olive gardens in the Kedron Valley, in at St. Stephen's Gate and home to Zion by the Via Dolorosa.

Sunday.

Service in the church on Mount Zion. The Creeds and the Te Deum were delightful there. It was indeed heart-stirring to say *there*,—

"*Thou art the King of glory, O Christ.*

"*When thou hadst overcome the sharpness of death, Thou didst open the kingdom of heaven to all believers.*

"*We therefore pray Thee, help Thy ser-*

vants: whom thou hast redeemed with Thy precious blood."

In the afternoon we walked alone, together, down Hinnom to the Hill of Evil Counsel. We climbed this, and sat with our English Bible near an ancient tomb in the hill-side, and looked on the rocky steeps and walls, and ploughed slopes of Zion. These were the really precious, never-to-be forgotten hours of our journeys in the Holy Land —hours which have made the Bible narratives to us for evermore not pictures merely, but solid realities which we have looked upon on many sides, and "our hands have handled."

Monday.

To-day we have had a splendid ride of eight or nine hours, round by Mizpeh (Nebi Samuel), Gibeon, Gibeah of Saul, Ramah and Anathoth. Our way led among the scenes of Samuel's life and of the early history of the kings; of Joshua's victory at Ajalon, and of Jonathan's heroic exploits. From

Nebi Samuel, the ancient Mizpeh, where Samuel judged the tribes, we had a noble view, extending from the Mediterranean to the blue Dead Sea. Far across the wide plain of Sharon a golden strip of sand marks the coast of the Mediterranean, lying far north, and interrupted here and there by intervening hills. Opposite rose the old fortress of Gibeon on the level summit of a round terraced hill. All around us surged wild stony moors and hills, a few grey olive-groves here and there suggesting what had been and might be.

Beautiful scarlet-blossomed pomegranates and mulberries grow near the wells. At Gibeon there is a fine spring in a cavern, below the "Pool of Joab." In the enclosure of an old mosque at Ramah, where Samuel lived, were an ancient well and tank—a stone on the mouth of one, the other open and dry. Broken columns were scattered around. We passed through Anatha, Jeremiah's Anathoth.

Some little every-day incidents are so interesting in the life of the people. At one well, at noon, in the broad valley below Ramah, the flocks were gathered to be watered—sheep, and goats, and kine—and shepherds waiting till the stone should be rolled from the well's mouth, and then each taking his turn.

We passed two or three threshing-floors—huge slabs of rock on the hill-sides, where four oxen were driven round and round, treading out the corn, now and then stopping, and stooping to eat a little grain, as they were not muzzled.

We rested, and fed the horses under some olives at Gibeah. The Bible was our companion everywhere, and we thought of Jonathan scaling the height and surprising the garrison of the Philistines, and of the day which strangely lingered once on Gibeon and Ajalon.

The country is very thinly peopled. In a ride of thirty miles, so near Jerusalem, we only passed four Arab villages, and those very poor; but, when every hill was terraced with pyramids and olive-gardens, and crowned with its white city or village, how different! We returned by the north side to Jerusalem, catching again that beautiful view of the city on the edge of its table-land, overhanging the Hinnom and Kedron valleys. There Jerusalem still has something of an imperial look.

The bimbashee, a rough soldier apparently, and rather embarrassed, and the Pasha, with his gentle polished manners, came successively to pay a visit to one of our party. There were sherbet and pipes, and complimentary speeches through an interpreter. Two or three of these Oriental visits were enough, but the very monotony of the salutations and compliments had an interest, as illustrating the Oriental manners of the Bible.

V.

The Plain of the Dead Sea.

WE are just returned from the most fatiguing journey we shall, in all probability, have to encounter, down to the burning desert plain of the Dead Sea,—a descent of nearly four thousand feet from Mount Zion, where I write; a descent not merely from the highlands to the sea-level, but from the hill-country of Judea into the oven-like Ghor or chasm of the Jordan, ending in the trough of the Dead Sea, unnaturally depressed thirteen hundred feet below the level of the Mediterranean. I will give you the substance of my notes as I took them on the journey.

The first night (*Tuesday, June* 10) we found our tents pitched in a wild nook of the hills outside the Greek convent of Marsaba Saba. We started in the afternoon about three hours before sunset, a party of six on horseback, including the dragoman and a German servant. The caravan, mules, tents, beds, provisions, muleteers, and cook had preceded us.

An Arab escort accompanied us, consisting of four Bedouin horsemen belonging to the tribes which infest the district we were to pass through. Our way at first led through the desolate valley of the Kedron, now dry. After passing the Pool of Siloam and the King's Gardens, all, hills and valleys alike, became bare and wild. It must be remembered that the epithets, "wild and uncultivated," convey very different ideas of scenery in our own land of temperate sun and abundant rains, and under the burning sun of a rainless Syrian summer. By wild hill country *we* mean uplands glowing with the gold and purple gorse and heather, or green and soft with short, crisp, grass—elastic turf over which the foot bounds without fatigue in the fresh mountain air—valleys where the full streams rush, bright as brown crystals over granite rocks—or, under the shade of tangled woods; we mean, indeed, turf and trees, and ferns and water, blue distances and fresh air—in short, embodied coolness of every kind, every thing which it is delightful to think of on a summer day. On the other hand, the wild hill-country we rode through when we left Jerusalem on that June afternoon, was a range of bare and lifeless rock, earth broken and baked into hard brown clods—hills glowing in yellow sunshine—valleys where the hill-shadows, when they fell, rested only on the rocky bed of the dry torrent. Cloud shadows there were none, and distances were distinguished as in a photograph, not by their color, but by their perspective. In that clear, disenchanting air the local color is scarcely changed by twenty miles of distance, and the local color every where is brown.

Above you, not sky and clouds, but light, unmitigated light; around you, not turf, and wood, and stream, and grey moss and lichen-covered rocks, but earth, earth, earth, brown earth and brown rock,—rich brown close to you, greyish brown in the shade, golden brown in the sunshine, amber brown in the distance. Thus in daylight I can never conceive the ordinary every-day aspects of the south to be as beautiful as those of our own temperate climes. But there are rare moments of startling gorgeous beauty here, before which the richest splendor of our sober north must seem pale and common-place,—sunsets, when the clouds, if there are any, seem, not illuminated, but steeped through and through with living light, when every point of the all pervading light seems clothed with color,—when prosaic, neutral tints seem banished from the glorified heavens and earth,—when shadows are of imperial purple, or of the rich brown of Venetian pictures—and every crevice, and crag, and shapeless clod seem gifted with definite and beautiful form—and the distances are like heaven—and sky like the Holy City, New

Jerusalem, whose streets are pure gold, as it were transparent glass, and her walls jasper, and her gates pearl. Something of this we saw that evening when the sun set behind the red hills of Moab, and even through the afternoon the mere vividness of the light, defining every object with exquisite clearness, was in itself a constant pleasure.

In one valley we passed some black Bedouin tents,—"tents of Kedar;" the dark camel's hair canvas stretched from pole to pole, and a few women and children stirring about the encampment.

The last part of the journey the scenery was very grand and strange. We rode through a magnificent wild gorge with parallel sides winding round for more than a mile. The sides were almost perpendicular cliffs, but sloped slightly in a series of rock-terraces some hundred feet down to the broad bed of a dry torrent. It was like a chasm forced by some great river, the Rhone, or Rhine; but all was dark, and dry, and silent. From a ledge, on one side of this gorge, rise the towers of the Marsaba Convent, almost as dreary and unhuman-looking as the gorge itself.

The rule of the convent forbids that women should be received as guests, and accordingly, as soon as our party appeared, two monks, who perceived us from a solitary tower which forms a kind of outpost of the monastery, began shouting a wild chant, which we supposed to be an exorcism of me. This weird chant, resounding from the sides, made the place seem more unearthly than before, and formed a fitting prelude to our entrance on those mysterious regions of death and doom which we were to traverse on the following day.

This chasm was once a favorite resort for hermits, and the rocks are pierced at all heights by the mouths of caverns which once were hermitages. Here numbers of human beings, about the fourth and fifth centuries, perhaps earlier, abandoned all God had given them of life, with the hope of thus drawing nearer himself.

So near the home at Bethany, and the open sepulchre of the Saviour, had Christianity found its way from the light of his Redeeming love into this chasm of death. So soon had the great enemy of man again woven his web of blinding falsehood over the character of God, and driven the bewildered soul into the wilderness to be tempted of him.

We were just in time to see that wonderful sunset burning over the hills of Moab on the other side of the Dead Sea, and gleaming with a capricious glow like the blaze of a conflagration, on the points of our tents, the edges of the convent roofs, the manes of our horses, and the spear-points of our four Bedouins, as they sat perched in a picturesque group on a point overlooking the gorge.

Then came the first entertaining experiences of the prolonged pic-nic of tent-life, with its Robinson Crusoe-like accommodations of things to all kinds of anomalous purposes, its freedom from the bondage of conventionality, and its bondage to the caprices of dragoman and muleteers.

The crescent moon rose as bright as a full harvest moon at home, and the stars were clear as if there had been no moon. All that night there was little sleep to be had, with the clanking of the chains around the fore-legs of our horses, occasionally the rubbing of their heads against the tent canvas close to one's face, and the endless chattering of the Arab escort who were couched around the camp-fire.

The next day (*Wednesday, June* 11) we started at half-past four in the morning, but we did not extricate ourselves from the labyrinth of wild ravines around Marsaba until the sun was intensely powerful. Then we had to cross the burning, shadeless plain, which stretched before us to the Dead Sea shore. The first half-hour of this day was occupied in retracing our steps through the strange Marsaba chasm, which looks as if it were a channel ready cut, and awaiting the advent of some stately river. In descending from this to the plain, we passed one singular hill, entirely of a strange ghostly white. Over the plain itself we then rode for some miles, the plain of the cities from which all human dwellings have vanished for thousands of years,—the plain which was the garden of Eden, now only dotted here and there along its dreary expanse with a few pale green shrubs, that seem rather to have the stony, unchanging half-life of corallines, than the fresh, varying, expanding life of plants—rather grey than green, with wiry stalks that have hardly energy to develope themselves into leaves.

When we reached the sea itself, my first feeling was a childish surprise that it looked so much like any other sea, blue and refreshing, with its waves sparkling and rippling against the shingly shore, as if it held in its depths all the marine abundance of animal and vegetable life, instead of rolling a lifeless mass of caustic water over the ruins of lost cities and the bones of lost men. Bible names and scenes are to us so typical, that one's first sensation on seeing the actual places, frequently is an unreasonable wonder at finding them so ordinary, and like other everyday places and things. I suppose, unconsciously, we had pictured that sea of death as a dark waste of waters breaking angrily against black cliffs, or heaving sullenly on a waste of sand, without troubling ourselves to inquire where the darkness and the shadows could come from. And there, on the contrary, it spread before us one expanse of sunny waters blue and sparkling, with little innocent ripples quietly bathing the shingly beach. Yet nevertheless it was as literally and fully a sea of death as ever we had imagined. Not a shell was ever thrown up on that shingle, not a fish lived in these bright waters, to the taste they were bitterd andacrid, a combination of pitch and salt, and those of our party who bathed there found the water so heavy that they floated almost like corks on it, and so caustic that it burned any scratch or cut very painfully.

After dismounting and resting a little while, we rode on again by the Dead Sea shore towards the mouth of the Jordan—a long, arid, weary, burning plain, or hollow, thirteen hundred feet below the Mediterranean. Every now and then, patches or dried up pools of salt, and tangled bundles of dead drift-wood, show the height to which the sea has risen during the "swellings of Jordan." A few scrubby, isolated shrubs pick up a living here and there, and even distil a fresh green from the sand and salt, but most even of the few dotted here and there, are of a dull, lifeless grey, with wiry, stalky leaves. There is nothing to interrupt one's meditations, or rather to weaken one's impressions (for conscious thought is too great an effort in the heat) of the terrible desolation of the scene, or to efface the lesson stamped on this lifeless sea and barren shore, that God's love involves at length a dreadful vengeance on those who pollute the world he loves with wrong and sin.

I shall never forget the delight with which, after riding on many weary miles along that salt and barren shore, we at length caught sight of the strip of real living green, the green of trees, which marks the Jordan, and heard the sound of its waters, real waters, not the mockery of that emblem of all that is living and life-giving, by whose side we had been plodding on so long, with burning faces and parched throats.

We pressed our tired horses on. It was indeed the Jordan, but not yet the place of our noon-day rest. We had to ride along the arc of another long winding of the river, and then in the shade of the wood or jungle which fringes the Jordan we found servants with bread, oranges, and all manner of refreshing things. The contrast was very pleasant. For a salt and sandy plain, where even the little grey shrubs dotted over it had been a relief from the glare,—a wood, a thicket of tangled boughs, and trees waving high above. For our failing supplies of tepid water, economised in niggardly sips from the earthen pitcher hot with the sun—a river, an abundant, rapid, generous river, rushing coolly over a rocky bed, with a sound like a Devonshire river,—no sluggish, canal-like stream, creeping noiselessly over an oozy bed, but a deep, broad current, flowing steadily and strong, and filling the air with its living voice.

The bed of the Jordan is very deep, and therefore, it fertilizes nothing beyond the little strip of wood on its banks. The point we were resting at was the traditional scene of the baptism of our Lord, to which the pilgrims throng in such numbers every year. The limestone hills close the river there into a ravine, and rise above the jungle abrupt as sea-cliffs, bare of any vegetation, burned to a rich warm tint by that almost tropical sun, and their stratification clearly visible. In some places tall reeds and canes grow on the edge of the water; in others, the trees overhang it; and at one point they enclose a sheltered nook where you can bathe, and have at once the inexpressible luxury of bathing your weary frame in the cool, soft, rapid stream, and your memory in all the associations of the place, till you could almost fancy that it was the virtue of the river itself which made Naaman's dips in it so miraculously healing, instead of the life-giving word which we know can make any instrument a means of life.

I rested in the thick of the wood, out of sight of the river, while the rest of the party bathed, and listened to the cool plashings of the water, the waters which had parted at the touch of the priests' feet for the sacred ark and of the hosts of Israel; also, centuries afterwards, where Jesus was baptized, and praying, the Holy Spirit descended on him like a dove.

After a short rest and refreshment we started again on our way to our encampment, which was to be at Elisha's Fountain, just beyond Jericho, at the foot of the hills which divide the Jordan valley from Jerusalem. We believed the distance to be short, and started in excellent spirits, although the sun was in his full strength; but the way seemed to lengthen out before us, as slowly we plodded on and across that burning-glass of a plain in the mid-day sun, without a feature to distinguish one weary mile from another—grey scrubby shrubs dotted unconnectedly over the great space of burning sand—no point of hope before us except the rampart of the Judæan hills gradually growing less faint.

At last we descried a white square tower in the distance with trees around it, and hoped it was in some way connected with Elisha's Fountain. The plain began to be a little less lifeless. The path descended into a wady. No stream was trickling at the bottom. Not even a stagnant pool remained, but the dried up rain torrent had left its traces in green trees and flowering shrubs, which seemed to us like the most beautiful garden. One of these shrubs had a pretty spikey blue flower, smelling sweetly. After this, two green hollows were passed on the right and left, then a little dell with an abundant stream flowing through it, which we hoped flowed from Elisha's Fountain. But the square tower proved not to be our resting place; we had been travelling since leaving the Jordan three or four hours, but we had further still to go. The white tower was in the poor Arab village which marks the site of Jericho. A few mean ruins are there and some trees, but not one palm where the city of palm trees stood.

At length we came to another green strip of life close under the hills, and there, among the thorny thickets, our white tents welcomed us, and the dragoman came out like a patriarch to greet us with refreshment. It was worth all the faintness and fatigue to enjoy that rest. The simple furniture of our tents was all arranged, and they looked quite home like already, whilst sherbet and tea consoled us for our long thirst.

Whilst resting quietly in our tent we heard a characteristic Oriental conversation in the next tent between an Arab sheikh and one of our party to whom he had come to pay his respects. The dragoman interpreted. The sheikh placed himself and all he possessed at our fellow-traveller's disposal, much in the same terms as Ephron the Hittite used towards Abraham; which proved in the end to mean that he would sell the services desired for twice their value, and on this being conceded he demanded a baksheesh. The bargain was then completed, and on the next day one member of our party was to venture alone with the sheikh into the country beyond Jordan, while the rest of us returned to Jerusalem.

After a short repose we walked to the Fountain of Elisha, or Ain es Sultan. It is a beautiful, abundant spring, welling up through the sand, pure and sweet, and clear —differing from the Jordan water, which, although sweet, is not clear, but thickened with the soft rocks it wears away. It is not a little bubbling spring, like the sources of many of our own rivers, but it rises to light from its deep reservoir under the hills—a large, limpid, lake-like pool, as broad as a full grown river, and flowing forth in two rapid musical streams in different directions. A building of large hewn stones had once enclosed it. Part of this had fallen in, in some places making the pool shallow and in others narrowing it. Large stones were scattered around. The fountain was a Hercules in its cradle, but strangled almost in its cradle by the serpents of lawlessness and indolence. A very short distance from its source this beautiful stream is evaporated by the sun, or swallowed up by the sand, and the life its beneficent waters cannot but create immediately around it is sadly illustrative of the thorns and thistles which the earth yields where man does not till it in the sweat of his brow. A day's labor of half a dozen Englishmen might clear the fountain, but there are none here but wandering Bedouins, and a few poor timid villagers on the height above, and nothing is ever repaired in this country. Thickets of thorny, fruitless bushes, or trees bearing only wild bitter fruit, fringe its banks, manifesting the vigor of their life chiefly in the malignant vigor of their long ruthless prickles. One large tree, however, shades it, and a few poor gardens of herbs are near, and altogether it will always remain in my memory as a picture of refreshment, coolness, shade, life, and everything that makes a contrast to the shadeless, treeless, lifeless, burning sand-wastes of the plain of the doomed cities and the Dead Sea.

Thursday, June 19.

The mountain range between Jericho and Jerusalem begins abruptly above Elisha's Fountain. One of our party has gone alone across the Jordan to the mountains of Moab with the Arabs, and two others are taking a morning ride to Jericho. I have been rambling quietly about and reading the Bible, and am now sitting under the shade of the prickly trees and shrubs, wood pigeons cooing among the bushes, picturesque Arabs chattering by the tents, the delicious music of Elisha's Fountain within hearing, and a breeze! These are delightful moments to remember.

As I sat quietly there, a woman brought some strange kind of grass which they use here instead of soap, and kneeling down on a stone in the brook wrapped up this grass in some soiled linen, and began pounding it clean with another stone. It reminded me of the laundresses beating the linen in their sheds by the Rhine at Cologne. The dragoman told me she was a Syrian Christian from Bethlehem.

JERUSALEM, *Friday, June* 20.

At eleven o'clock I started with the dragoman on the long ascent from Jericho to Jerusalem, leaving the gentlemen to bathe in Elisha's Fountain.

It is a long, toilsome ascent up rocky stairs along the sides of dreary brown ravines, rifted and scarred by the violent winter torrents, with a few dry stunted shrubs dotted about the burnt up earth. It is most unusually void of feature and picturesque interest for a mountain path, but we had at different points two fine views of the Dead Sea, glittering beneath us far across the desert plain at the base of the hills of Moab. The sun beat on us as in a furnace reflected by the heated rocks, the ascents were precipitous, the horses could or would only creep slowly along, and the journey altogether took us seven hours.

Midway we reached the great ruined khan, where tradition says the Good Sarmaritan housed the man who fell among thieves on this road. This localizing of the parable is less absurd than at first it might seem. That parable is more an illustrative anecdote than strictly a parable. Our Lord himself gives the narrative a definite location, and the scenery remains in every respect unchanged from that day to this. The inn is there, the only house between Jericho and Bethany; the lonely road is there, and the thieves are certainly there. Three or four very questionable-looking Bedouins rode up to us, two of them at a time, and when they saw our Arab escort, turned aside and amused themselves with laughing and levelling their spears at us to signify what they could do. The khan is a great ruined building, probably never more than a mere shelter, and now not even that. A large platform is scooped out near it from the rocky side of the hill, bounded by a low wall, and on this we sat half an hour and rested. We saw the black mouth of a cave in the opposite hill. Perhaps this was once a resort for hermits or recluses.

When we remounted our horses the ascent became rather less steep, and just after we left the khan, a delicious reviving breeze from the West met us, one of the mountain breezes which daily refresh the mountain city of Jerusalem. In a valley some way further on, we came to a well which our Arab guide called the Well of Moses. It was dry, except a tiny thread of bad water trickling over a slimy spout, with a green pool beside it, from which even our tired and thirsty horses turned away in disgust. Thence we still climbed on and on, over hill after hill, on that long ascent; but now the air was that of the Land of Promise, not that of the doomed plain, breezy and pure, whilst the scenery, though not less wild, was more picturesque, crags rising from the hills, and boulders strewn around, and scanty rock vegetation occasionally tinging the earth a welcome green. Thus at last we came to the rocky threshing-floors, and low, rough cabins of Bethany, and passed on amongst its stone huts, and then looked back on its lovely olive clad valley, with the blue hills of Moab beyond. Above, again, the road winds up to cross a shoulder of the Mount of Olives, and we were on the point where some think our Lord stood when he last led the disciples "as far as to Bethany, and ascended blessing them," through this pure air till the cloud received him out of their sight. A little beyond this the white minarets and domes of Jerusalem gleam on the sight, above a depression of Olivet as you "draw nigh the city." Again we lost them in the next slight descent, until at the next ascent that sudden view of the whole city burst upon us which has been described—the steep sides of Moriah once crowned with the temple, and backed by the palaces on the further and higher crest of Zion. "And when he beheld the city" hence, "he wept over it." We entered Jerusalem by St Stephen's Gate, and were thankful when, after stumbling and scrambling over the lumps of marble polished by the tread of centuries, which pave the narrow dirty street, we alighted from our tired horses on Mount Zion.

But all the dreary way our thoughts kept recurring to our Saviour's last journey from beyond the Jordan to Bethany, when after those "two days" which explain so many a delayed answer to prayer, he came at the call of the sister, and brought with him, in himself, life and resurrection.

And He, as we often thought when fatigue with our long day's journeys, came all the dreary road on foot. One would not wish to travel in the Holy Land without experiencing something of weariness and thirst, and the burden and heat of the day.

VI.

The Mount of Olives.

ON Friday the 13th June we rested in Jerusalem. The expedition to the Red Sea had tired us much, and in such a country days of absolute rest are as precious as they are necessary. It is delightful to be relieved for a while from the hurry of doing as much as possible, and the responsibility of seeing as much as possible, and just to be quiet, and realize that we are here, in the Holy Land, in Jerusalem, while the fingers are busy drawing and sketching; to go in and out among the sacred names, and acquire a kind of everyday familiarity with the sacred places by the associations of everyday life; to cease to be a sight seer, and become, if only for a few hours, a dweller among the old, familiar hallowed scenes. For in the ordinary occupations of daily life there is nothing incongruous with the associations of our faith. The ties that bind us to our sacred histories are no flimsy gossamer of devotional sentiment, which a breath of morning air may blow away, but heart ties, which familiarity only strengthens ; and what we want to feel is, how everyday the world, and the life, and the men of Bible times were—how like our own—how like ourselves. "Count it not strange as though some strange thing happened unto you ;" "Men of like passions with ourselves," is written on every page of that most divine and most human Book, except of One, and of him it is written, "He came eating and drinking," hungering and thirsting, journeying and sleeping, and was in all points tempted as we are, "*yet without sin.*" It is the very familiarity of the scenes and circumstances which detaches into glorious distinctness that spotless character, and yet brings His words and presence home to us with such sustaining power in our own daily life.

Friday being the Mohammedan Sabbath, the gates of Jerusalem were closed at mid-day, whilst the muezzin's call to prayers resounded from the minaret, recalling the long ages of romantic conflict in crusading times, and ringing like a death knell over the desecrated city, repeating from day to day the doom, "Trodden under foot of the Gentiles."

Yet the city is scarcely as much desecrated now as in the days when scribes and Pharisees, Sadducees and Herodians were its religious men, and Pontius Pilate and Annas the high priest its rulers. We thought of this as we left the city on Saturday evening, [June 14th] to remain a day or two on the Mount of Olives. The Mount of Olives and the Sea of Galilee had been always the two places in the Holy Land I had most longed to see. And now we were going out of Jerusalem to pass a night on Olivet.

We went out at the Zion gate, and walked round the outside of the Haram, or sacred enclosure, which we had gone over within some days previously. We passed close under the fragment of the walls at the east end of the temple area, which were the ancient fortifications of the city; the stones are very large, like those from which the arch of the bridge between Moriah and Zion sprang. Of the Temple itself, we know, not one stone was left on another. The way led by the Golden Gate, a gate no longer, but a walled up gateway, where the old arches rise above the rough masonry which fills them up, a monument of Moslem superstition, and of the fears of a religion whose faith is not in itself, but in the swords that defend it.

Not far beyond this, the path from the Zion gate joins that from the St. Stephen's Gate, and leads down the steep sides of Moriah to the bridge of the Kedron.

Almost every point of the topography of Jerusalem has been, or is, a point of warm debate, especially (as every one knows,) the situation of Calvary. Some believe that the spur of Moriah, where the paths from the

Zion and St. Stephen's Gate, after uniting, descend to the bed of the Kedron, is Calvary. To us it was always an endeavor while on the spot to avoid perplexing ourselves with discussions about uncertain sites. The certain features of the scenes were so many and so absorbing and the interest of the general landscape so far greater than precise accuracy as to a few yards of ground, that we took care not to confuse our recollections of the whole scene by entering into discussions as to the exact site of particular events. But this spur of Moriah was so often in our sight, we passed over it so frequently in leaving and re-entering the city, and became so familiar with it during our little sojourn opposite it on Olivet, that it may be well briefly to state a few of the reasons which have led some Bible topographers to fix on it as the scene of the crucifixion rather than the site of the Church of the Holy Sepulchre.

In the first place, This point must always have been outside the line of the city walls, which many doubt if the traditional site of the holy sepulchre could ever have been.

Secondly, It is at the same time so close to the city, that priests and Levites standing on the walls of the Temple area, without ceremonially defiling themselves by mingling with a crowd attending an execution, might have seen and heard all that happened.

Thirdly, It is, and always must have been, close to a frequented highway—the road to Bethany, Jericho, and through the Valley of the Kedron in either direction to the south or north. It is difficult to realize that any thing went on as usual on that awful day; yet we know that many, perhaps most, men must have been going about their usual pursuits; and that besides "the people that came together to that sight," there were many who "passed by and railed on him, wagging their heads," as they looked up to the Temple whose destruction he had prophesied standing close at hand in all its strength and glory, and then to him agonizing on the shameful cross, and then proceeded on their daily errands to Bethany or Siloam, just as men of another race do at this day.

Fourthly, All his acquaintance, and the women who followed him from Galilee, could have stood "afar off" across the Kedron valley on the Mount of Olives, quite out of reach of the jeers of that mocking crowd, and yet have "beheld all these things" in every detail.

Fifthly, The place was a Golgotha, the place of a skull, and if the common acceptation given to that term is right, it is equally applicable to this spur of Moriah now. Bones and refuse are scattered about it.

Sixthly, "In the place where He was crucified there was a garden," and on this spot there is a garden at this day—a garden and tombs.

This point must, no doubt, remain uncertain ; but in reading again and again the story of the cross, that story of Moriah, with its tombs and gardens underneath the Temple walls, looking across Gethsemane to the Mount of Olives, with the road to Bethany passing by it, rises naturally before my mind as the scene where the Cross was raised. Its being a part of Moriah, moreover, gives probability to this view on typical grounds, since thus the Moriah where God provided the lamb instead of Isaac would indeed be the very spot where the Lamb of God, without blemish and without spot, gave himself for us.

It is remarkable that the expression "mount," so perpetually applied to Calvary, and perpetuated by James Montgomery in his touching hymn on the three sacred mountains, occurs nowhere in the New Testament.

Much of this formed the subject of our conversation as we walked down the steep path to the bridge over the Kedron. The bed of the torrent was dry, but the bridge remained to indicate its force and breadth in the rainy season. It was evening.

"And in the day time he was teaching in the temple, and at night he went out and abode in the mount that is called the Mount of Olives." How often, just as the shadows were falling as now over us, and all the hill and valley lying dim except the highest point of Olivet, which glowed in the golden light of the sun setting behind the city, had our Saviour's feet trodden that very pathway.

"And every man went unto his own house. Jesus went unto the Mount of Olives," not as we were going, to the shelter of a friendly roof, but to pass whole nights in prayer among the solitudes of that olive-clothed valley, "whither he oftentimes resorted." We were entering the very sanctuary of his earthly life, the place where he prayed to his Father in secret—such prayer as the 17th of John gives us a glimpse into.

About half way up the Mount of Olives we branched off from the road to Bethany to the tower whose owner had so hospitably offered to receive us. It was a rough, narrow tower, something in the style of one of the small Border fortresses, or like a tower in a vineyard, a lodge in a "garden of cucumbers." [Cucumbers, or vegetable marrows, eaten raw, form, we were told, a large portion of the food of the peasants during the intervals of the harvests.]

The lower story was a kitchen and a stable with a mere loophole to admit light. Outside the door of this a stone staircase led to the first floor, where were the bedroom in which we slept and the sitting room looking toward the city. Above were two small bedrooms, and then the flat roof, commanding a very fine view. There we were domiciled for two most happy days, richer in recollections to me than any we spent in the Holy Land, except two or three by the Sea of Galilee. It is difficult to convey their impressions to others. It *was just being there*, and that is much to remember, although little to say.

We took the Sunday literally and conscientiously as a Sabbath—a day of rest—in consideration of fatigues past and future.

In the early morning we saw the first sunbeams from the eastern sky behind us light up the walls and white domes and housetops of Jerusalem, and creep slowly down the sides of Moriah to the valley of Jehoshaphat. Then, alone, we wandered quietly up to the top of the hill, to look across the wild hills we had travelled over between Jerusalem and Jericho, to the Dead Sea, glittering at the foot of the mountains of Moab. Afterwards we descended Olivet by the footpath to Bethany, by the bright green wild fig trees, and the grey olives which shade it here and there, to the valley of the Kedron. We saw the Greek Church which is said to contain the tomb of the Virgin, and the white walls of the Latin Garden of Gethsemane, near which the Greeks are establishing another Gethsemane in order that their pilgrims may have equal advantages with those of the Latin Church. How quickly we passed by these things, which, if possible, would reduce these sacred scenes to the level of Loretto or the Holy Coat of Treves, you can imagine. They were soon lost sight of, and then we were alone again in the quiet valley, in some retreat of which Gethsemane most certainly was, perhaps in the solitary nook where we sate out of sight, though within sound of the city.

There we rested under the shade of the old olives, with their gnarled black trunks and light leaves. Pomegranates, with their scarlet blossoms, and fig-trees, were scattered here and there; and perhaps the garden whose name is so sacred to us was little more than that.

As it was chosen for a retreat—a place of rest and solitude—it seems more probable that it would be in some winding of the valley such as that we were in, out of sight of ordinary passers-by, than at the junction of the roads where the white walls of the Latin traditional Gethsemane rise. But such discussions did not disturb our minds, as we rested there alone on that bright Sunday morning. We were too surely near the place where, "being in agony, he prayed the more earnestly," and said, "Not my will, but thine be done," to think of anything but that.

"Though
Fast as evening sunbeams by the sea,
  Thy footsteps all in Sion's deep decay
Were blotted from the holy ground; yet dear
Is every stone of hers, for Thou wert surely here.

There is a spot within this sacred dale
  That felt Thee kneeling, touched thy prostrate brow.
One angel knows it. Oh, might prayer avail
  To win that knowledge! Sure each holy vow
Less quickly from the unstable soul would fade,
Offered where Christ in agony was laid.

Might tear of ours once mingle with the blood
  That from His aching brow by moonlight fell,
Over the mournful joy our thoughts would brood,
  Till they had framed within a guardian spell
To chase repining fancies, as they rise,
Like birds of evil wing, to mar our sacrifice.

So dreams the heart, self-flattering, fondly dreams;
  Else wherefore, when the bitter waves o'erflow,
Miss we the light, Gethsemane, that streams
  From thy dear name, where in His page of woe
It shines, a pale, kind star in winter's sky?
Who vainly reads it there, in vain had seen Him die."

We reascended the hill, across its terraced

sides, to our tower, to rest from the heat of the noon-day sun under the shade of its thick stone walls. There we dined alone on cold meat, bread, and dried fruits we had brought from the city, and had a delicious quiet time, reading in the Psalms and Prophets and the Gospels all we could find about the scenes we were in the midst of, and thinking of all at home. We wrote letters, also, to some schools at home, in which we thought the children would attach a special value to a few words actually written on the Mount of Olives; and as we talked and wrote, or sat in happy silence, Jerusalem rose before us across the valley of the Kedron, whilst beneath us fell the sunny slopes of Olivet, dotted here and there with grey olives, fresh green fig-trees, and bright, blossoming pomegranates, each casting its distinct and individual shadow on the warm brown earth, and silently photographing gospel narratives and parables on our mind.

From the window we watched, also, for some time, a shepherd slowly pacing down across the hill before his flock, with a staff in his hand. It was a mixed flock of sheep and goats, and as they strayed hither and thither, though never far from his footsteps, or lingered to crop the scanty herbage or the lower leaves of the shrubs, from time to time he would call them on, and the "sheep knew his voice and followed him." It was as if the words of the parables had suddenly become things, and passed in a series of living pictures before us.

In the evening we walked to the heights above Bethany with the rest of our party, who had returned from Jerusalem to see the sunset reflected on the hills of Moab. The point which we reached was a breezy, rocky height, which in England would be a grassy heath, just beyond the summit of the Mount of Olives, out of sight of Jerusalem, and overlooking Bethany, so that many think it peculiarly corresponds to the two facts mentioned to determine the scene of the Ascension: "He led them out as far as to Bethany," and "then returned they to Jerusalem from the mount called Olivet." If so, it was here on these quiet, breezy heights that the great miracle was wrought which, as has been said, in its majestic simplicity makes even the pomp of Elijah's fiery chariot poor in comparison:—One in human form, by his inherent power overcoming all the laws of the planetary systems, and rising untouched and unattended into the heaven He left to save man.

Bethany was little to the disciples then. Their eyes were far above its olives and white-roofed houses, strained upward to pierce the cloud which hid their Master from their sight. The gospel history was finished. No longer was Nazareth, or Bethany, or Jerusalem, or Olivet the abode of Jesus, but heaven. The gospel histories were finished, and the history of the Church was beginning. "Why stand ye gazing up into heaven?" sent the apostles back to Jerusalem to live that foundation and type of all Church history recorded in the Acts of the Apostles.

On our way back to the tower we met a

shepherd carrying a sick lamb on his shoulder; and with this second parable, our Sunday in the Mount of Olives closed.

Early on Monday morning (June 16), we went once more alone to that sacred height above Bethany, to see the sun rise once more behind the hills of Moab, and to sketch. I feel as if I knew Bethany and the heights around it quite well. Beautiful, breezy hills they are, with slabs of rock tufted with herbage, reminding us of English downs. The valley on the slopes of which Bethany stands is really lovely—full of grey olives, among which the few pomegranates and figs which grow here and there, look like the fresh green forest trees in spring amongst dull firs and evergreens. Beyond surge the desolate hills between Jerusalem and Jericho; and beyond again, like a sapphire wall at that early hour, rose the hills of Moab, with the bright line of the Dead Sea just visible at their feet.

The village is very wretched. The dark, rough, flat-roofed hovels looked little like

A Well near Bethany.

homes. Dogs barked furiously at us from their roofs when we passed through. They are, however, not more miserable than Connemara cabins, and, at all events, there are no pigs, and there is no mud from rain. But certainly there is not a house one could imagine to have been like Martha and Mary's, or one in which you could fancy they could have made our Lord a supper. Yet here that supper was made, one of the few feasts our earth had for her Lord, where Martha served, and Lazarus, "which had been dead," sat at meat, and Mary broke the alabaster vase of precious ointment, which perfumes her name and the name of Bethany, to all generations, with the fragrance of gratitude and love, so rarely lavished on Him.

Still the hills, and the quiet valley, and the distant mountain range, and the breezy paths over the rocky slopes of Olivet are the very same. An old ruined castle stands at one entrance of the village, built partly of very large, ancient stones. Perhaps these belonged to some of the houses of the old Jewish village; perhaps even to the house whose sorrows and joys are so familiar to us. In all the Holy Land there cannot be a place of deeper and happier interest; and we may well be content that the stones of the earthly dwelling should be scattered, we who hope one day to see its blessed inmates, and to dwell with Martha and Mary and Lazarus in the city which hath foundations,—in the home of "Him who is the life indeed."

VII.

The Two Valleys—

HINNOM AND JEHOSHAPHAT.

IT was pleasant to return to our cool rooms in Simeon Rosenthal's hotel on Mount Zion after leaving Bethany and the Mount of Olives. The entrance to our inn was through a courtyard, where we always dismounted at the foot of a rude flight of stone steps, which led over the flat roofs of the lower rooms to the vaulted hall where we took our meals. This room had a window looking over the city. Pigeons ventured near sometimes, and perched on the window sill, and three times a day a cool reviving breeze came in from the sea or the mountains. A little beyond the door of the sitting-room two or three steps descended through a door in a low wall into a garden on a lower roof, from which an arched door-way opened into our bedroom, another large, airy room, with thick walls, and one of those cool, vaulted roofs which form the domes so characteristic of the cities in the south of Palestine. These rooms were furnished much in the same way as in a moderate German hotel. Above them rose one higher roof, from which we had our first view, over the roofs of Jerusalem, of the Temple precincts, thence of the large open reservoirs beside them, and the three brown summits of the Mount of Olives beyond. And now the names so familiar to our hearts had become pictures familiar to our eyes. It is difficult to give any idea of the charm of feeling these sacred names becoming everyday realities—solid, actual, familiar things blended with daily life—and thus giving in our minds a deeper reality, and therefore a tenderer sacredness, to the great events and the holy presence which have consecrated them.

In the afternoon we called on Miss Cooper at her Industrial School for Jewesses, and then went out by St. Stephen's Gate, and, descending into the Kedron Valley, took the path towards the village of Siloam. We passed the curious pyramidal mausoleum, half hewn out of the rock and half built on it, called the tomb of Absalom, on which it is a traditional custom for the wayfarer to cast a stone as he passes, in token of his detestation of Absalom's undutiful rebellion. The strength and endurance of the tradition says much for the impression made by the family order and reverence so deeply stamped on the Bible. The fact of that sad history of filial ingratitude and punishment has been so strongly felt that tradition has had to find it a locality, and has given it possession of one of the many unknown and empty tombs which surround the fallen city.

Other massive rock-hewn mausoleums are

beside Absalom's Tomb, and the sides of the valley everywhere, especially at this its narrowest part, were pierced with the cave-tombs of many races. If everywhere it is true that the dead laid beneath the soil far outnumber the living who tread it, a hundredfold is this the case with Jerusalem. Now a poor, thinly-peopled Turkish town, once the royal, the sacred city of a prosperous nation, the bones of kings and warriors, of the slain of five besieging armies and their victims, mingle of the dust of her hills and valleys. And, besides this, the tradition of the Moslem religion, so long dominant in the East, coincides with the faith of the Jew in fixing the Valley of Jehoshaphat as the scene of the final judgment, and thus makes it a favorite burial-ground for both. The ignorant Jew, it is said, believes that, as all are to rise in this place, the bodies of the dead will have to work their way underground like moles from their various burial-places to the sides of the Mount of Olives, and therefore many an aged Jew will totter to Jerusalem to die, preferring to perform this inevitable journey at any cost in this life, rather than after death. Moslem's eyes are fixed on the broken column projecting from the walls of the Temple enclosure over the Kedron Valley, as Mohammed's throne of judgment. But, whether led by wild and grovelling traditions, by a false sacred book, or by the inspired pages of Divine prophecy, on this valley, on these slopes, the gaze of the followers of the three religions is fixed, expecting that sacred feet are to stand again on the Mount of Olives, that all nations shall be gathered here to judgment, and this lonely, desolate valley of the dead be thronged with eager, trembling life. "Multitudes, multitudes in the valley of decision"—in *this* valley of the judgment of God, Jehoshaphat! Whatever differences may exist among Christians as to prophetical interpretation, nothing can lessen the solemnity which invests the only place in the world to which the minds of Jews, Mohammedans, and Christians turn with equal interest and the same overwhelming anticipation.

From the Valley of the Kedron we ascended the desolate slopes of Mount Zion, a strange scramble over ploughed fields and among old, dry wells, tombs and pits, which made it necessary to walk very warily. From this waste, uninhabited side of the old royal hill we looked across the ravine of Hinnom to the Hill of Evil Counsel, with its craggy sides and cave tombs. Tradition marks this as the death-place of the traitor Judas. On the other side the green gardens of the king lay beneath us, below the "Pool of Siloam," and above, beyond the many foldings of the brown intervening hills, rose the blue mountains of Moab.

We began to know our way quite well about the neighborhood of Jerusalem. It was remarkable how our interest deepened in proportion to our familiarity with the scenes, as in some measure we passed out of the condition of sight-seers, with every sense alert for novelties, into the quieter frame of ordinary inhabitants.

This Valley of Hinnom we had more than once traversed, painfully toiling through the track paved with a deep mass of loose stones, which forms its only road, from its head, near the Jaffa Gate, to its junction with the Valley of Jehoshaphat at the steepest angle of Moriah. The upper part is called the Valley of Gihon, and commences in a slight depression of the table land at the west of the city, gradually deepening into a narrow, shady ravine beneath Zion and Moriah. At the head are a series of three large tanks or reservoirs, in successive stages, excavated in the rock. It is supposed these were the Pools of Gihon; they were now quite dry. The lower part of the valley is precipitous; its craggy sides are caverned with tombs, and opposite Zion it is hemmed in by the Hill of Evil Counsel, haunted with the terrible memory of Aceldama.

It is a remarkable thing, even in this wonderful allegorical land, that the Holy City should be fenced on two sides by valleys, one of which is looked on by the adherents of three religions as the scene of the final judgment, whilst the name of the other is used by our Lord himself to indicate the place of final doom*—Jehoshaphat and Gehenna.

Strangely different are the associations of these two valleys. The valley of Kedron, linked with tenderest and most solemn memories in the earthly life of our Lord, watered by the brook over which he so often passed on his way to Bethany: once crossed by the joyous throng hailing his triumphal entry into Jerusalem, made glad with children's hosannas, and strewn with festive palms and garments; and, more than all, hiding somewhere in its tranquil bosom the garden of his frequent prayers and his midnight agony.

The Valley of Hinnom, on the other hand, black with the darkest associations of the

* Mathew v. 22 (Greek).

cruel heathenism adopted by the Jews from the earliest races of Canaan, echoing to all time with the piteous wails of the little children burned alive in its gloomy depths, the cries of the victims having been drowned at intervals by the tabrets of the priests and worshippers collected in its groves. In the days succeeding the captivity, when Pagan idolatry ceased to be the sin of the Jewish nation, horror at its past scenes of torture and crime made it a place it seemed reverence to desecrate. The bodies of malefactors and the carcases of animals were thrown into it; and, to prevent its polluted air infecting the city, funeral fires burned there night and day. Thus Gehenna, the ravine of Hinnom, with its terrific images of continual corruption and unquenched fires, is used by our Lord himself as the type of that place where their worm dieth not and their fire is not quenched.

Imagine a Christian of Apostolic times standing at the angle on Mount Zion on which we stood, and in one glance sweeping those two valleys: the ravine of Hinnom on one side, glaring with its fearful fires, made typical by the voice of Him who, knowing the terrible abysses which skirt our mortal life, deemed it the highest compassion to unveil them; with the dreadful story of Judas haunting its precipitous sides—Gehenna, the dark valley of the shadow of the second death: on the other side the Valley of the Kedron, sacred with the memories of redemption, the nights of the Saviour's prayer, the garden of his redeeming agony, where he tasted how bitter the cup of our curse was, and held it fast, and drank it to the dregs—the scene, perhaps, of his future manifestation in glory, when his feet should stand on the Mount of Olives. Then think with what feelings such a Christian would return to the city, to plead with the multitudes there for whom the Redeemer's tears had fallen and his blood had been shed, to turn from the doom so certain and so fearfully pictured, to the salvation also so certain, so dearly bought, so free to all who would listen and believe.

And do not we Christians of these days all stand, as it were, at such an angle of the City of God, with judgment and redemption as plainly in our sight? And shall we be less earnest?

One strong contrast between Oriental and European cities must strike all Eastern travellers, and this is especially the case with Jerusalem. There are no suburbs. There is no easy intermingling with town and country life,—the city overflowing into the country in villas and suburban villages, the country blending with the city in market-gardens, parks, and groves. Immediately outside the gates of Jerusalem you are in a solitude, almost in a desert. Pits, and ruins, and heaps of rubbish lie on all sides, wild Bedouins meet you, and neglected wastes surround you. In some measure this must, of course, be the result of bad government, the insecurity of life, which compels men to seek the defence of numbers, and the insecurity of property which paralyzes industry. Yet there are traces in the Bible of a similar state of things, partly, no doubt, from similar causes, but partly, also, to be attributed to the hilly nature of the country. Close to the Jaffa Gate were deep, unguarded pits, and one very deep one especially, which often reminded us of the danger which our Lord appealed to as so familiar to the Pharisee who sought to entangle him. "If any of you have on ox or an ass, and it fall into a pit," was a catastrophe evidently as common in those days as it must be now. The cement which lines an underground water tank cracks, and becomes a broken cistern, and is abandoned, leaving its open mouth a snare to all unwary animals; wells are dried up with the same result.

Evidently, also, a few minutes sufficed to bring our Saviour to those "desert places" which he so habitually sought for prayer, thus practically proving to us that no abstraction of mind will compensate for being absolutely and consciously alone with God in secret prayer, when that is possible.

This was our last walk in the neighborhood of Jerusalem, our last survey of the two valleys of doom and redemption, of Gehenna and Gethsemane, which so mystically skirt the earthly Jerusalem, "the city of the great King."

VIII.

Solomon's Gardens,

HEBRON, AND BETHLEHEM.

ON Tuesday, June 17th, we set off for the hill-country of Judea, Hebron and Bethlehem. It was to be a three days' excursion, and much for us depended on the way in which it was carried out, as the success of this expedition was to decide whether we should afterwards attempt the longer tour through Northern Palestine. We started in excellent spirits, although not with the best horses in the world. The master of our hotel was our dragoman. The air was light and fresh with the pure morning breeze, and all promised well.

We walked to the Jaffa Gate by Miss Cooper's industrial school, where we saw her

Jewesses seated on low divans round the rooms, happily occupied in sewing, weaving, and making twine.*

At the Jaffa Gate we met our horses, muleteers, and baggage, with the English Consul and Mrs. Finn, who had very kindly undertaken to introduce us to Solomon's Gardens at Urtass—a place in which they took especial interest, on account of the model farm lately commenced there with the object of affording employment to Jewish converts.

We were entering David's country. The incidents of his life, with its strong contrasts of lowliness and grandeur, joy and sorrow, were entwined with the name of almost every town and village, hill and valley, cave and desert we saw. We were leaving Jerusalem, where the words and deeds of three

* Information on missionary subjects has, for the most part, been omitted from these notes, because the intervening years have, of course, made any such information out of date.

years, and more especially the words and deeds of three days, of incarnate Godhead made all other associations sink into insignificance, except as connected with them, for a portion of the Holy Land rich in Old Testament memories, but linked to the New Testament only by the sacred name of Bethlehem, and the journey of the virgin mother to that hill-country of Judea which we were now traversing.

Was Hebron, the Levitical city, the City of Refuge, the home of Zacharias and Elisabeth? Then the footsteps of Mary must have passed across these very hills. Alone, in the guardianship of God and his angels, with the hope of the world in her heart, and in hers alone of all human beings, she crossed these hills, lonely, no doubt, then in many places, though not with the dead solitude of to-day, to meet the one other woman whom God gave her to share the wondrous secret of her joy.

Una and her lion, Milton's picture of the majesty of purity in Comus, and all other images of purity, tenderness and courage, seem rough and poor beside that maiden of Galilee fearlessly pursuing her quiet, unnoticed way,—

> "Tracing huge forests and unharbored heaths,
> Infamous hills, and sandy, perilous wilds,"—

to the mother of the Baptist. Let us not desecrate it by any mediæval allegorizing. No lilies sprang in her path, no millennial lambs did her homage, no glory shone around her. But God was with her,—

> "A thousand liveried angels lacqueyed her,
> Driving far off each thing of sin and guilt;"

and all along the solitary way her lowly and happy soul magnified the Lord, and her spirit rejoiced in God her Saviour. Well, indeed, may we in these latter generations call her "*blessed*," for from the heavens where she rests the word comes back to us from the lips of her Saviour and ours—comes back individually to each one of us who love him, sealed with a richer beatitude than even hers as his mortal mother—sealed with a "yea," and multiplied with a "rather": "Yea, rather, blessed are those who hear the word of God, and keep it." And looking round about on the disciples, with that comprehensive, yet most individualizing glance which St. Mark records, he said, "Behold my mother and my brethren."

That morning ride across the breezy hills was very inspiriting. We crossed more than once one of Solomon's aqueducts, a covered channel which conveyed the waters from the neighboring hills into Jerusalem. In many places the stones which roof the channel are broken in, and the shepherds water their flocks at the stream which still flows there.

We passed one of the many places in this country sacred alike to Jew and Mohammedan, and fraught with a tender interest to the Christian,—Rachel's tomb. It is now a massive, solitary mosque, jealously guarded from intrusion ; but below it is a cave—probably the original cave-tomb of Rachel—into the interior of which you may peep through a small opening, although you may by no means enter. Except for its desolation and melancholy solitude, there is little in it to harmonize with one of the tenderest histories of human love and sorrow in the Old Testament. How close home to the heart that narrative comes amidst all the old-world histories of violence, and feuds, and petty war fares between tribes which were the germs of nations! Amidst so much that is foreign to our life and thoughts, this history is fresh and heart-touching as if it had happened in the immediate circle of our friends.

It is as if amidst one of the old, deserted, giant cities, with their massive walls and Cyclopean temples, and traces of war and savage worship, we suddenly came on a home strewn with the traces of recent everyday occupations, household vessels, children's toys, pillows retaining the impress of the head that lay there yesterday, and wet with the tears of mourners. It is the one sanctuary of uncalculating and self-sacrificing affection, unsullied by the low and covetous aims which debased so much of Jacob's life. For her sake the seven years of service seemed nothing to him for the love he had to her. It was an intense personal affection, independent of all cost and all consequences. Dearer to him alone than all on earth beside, her children seem to have been dear to him more for her sake than even for their own. "He alone is left of his mother, and his father loveth him," was the plea for Benjamin with Joseph. Then what could exceed the pathos of Rachel's own history, the southern fervor of her character, the death caused by the very fulfilment of her passionate desire? And afterwards the dying mother's name of sorrow changed by the father into the name of tenderness, the son of her anguish into the son of his right hand; the tender minuteness with which, long years afterwards, Jacob digresses from the blessing of Joseph's children to the mother's death: "And as for me, when I came from Padan, Rachel died by me in land of Canaan, in the way, when yet there was but a little way to come unto Ephrath;" the kind of fond, motherly pride, which made the father clothe the motherless boy in the coat of many colors—all these tender touches which linger around every memory of the beloved wife, do they not show that God melted Jacob's heart through human love as well as by divine revelation? The angel who was more than angelic surely wrestled with Jacob at other places besides Peniel, giving divine strength to so many since Jacob, by that very touch which seemed to take all strength away. Surely that death and that tomb by the wayside brought the bereaved into the presence of God as well as Bethel and Peniel; and He whose love includes in its depths all that is highest and tenderest in the love of father, mother, or husband, taught Jacob much through that love and sorrow.

It seemed a cold and lifeless monument to such a history, that shapeless, solitary building. A mound of earth, or a tree, which spring would have renewed every year, and made the cradle of flowers or the home of birds, would have seemed more in harmony with that simple narrative of love, and life, and death.

We reached Urtass before midday—the valley of Solomon's Gardens. As to the economical value of this farm as a missionary experiment I can offer no opinion, but its value to us was very great as a *restoration* of the Bible pictures of the Holy Land in its days of glory and beauty. Such as this valley is, the whole land in its peopled and cultivated portions must have been—a land not only flowing with milk and honey from the upland pastures, and the breezy, thyme scented hills, but "a land of wheat, and barley, and vines, and fig trees, and pomegranates—a land of oil and olive"—a "land of fountains and depths which spring out of valleys and hills"—a "land of hills and valleys which drinketh water of the rain of heaven."

The farm house (Meshullam's) was situated in a quiet nook, low in the valley. We had our cold luncheon on stone seats in the shade of a tree outside the house, which was not unlike an Italian farm house. Our friends guided us up the hillsides, which were very steep, but irregularly terraced. Every level bit was covered with vines. The bright, fresh green of the luxuriant vine leaves was very refreshing to the eye after the brown, burnt-up hills around Jerusalem. These vines need no artificial watering. The rains of the rainy season, and afterwards the heavy night dews of the dry season, keep them juicy and vigorous, As we climbed the hills we continually came on the roots and stumps of old oaks, terebinths, &c. sprouting healthily with fresh leaves. These, with fig trees and vines, grow to the summit of the hills. The improvident peasantry think nothing, we were told, of destroying trees to make charcoal, and thus the country is steadily laid waste. But the old, gnarled roots were there to tell their tale of noble trunks and canopies of leafy branches, once filling the valley with the music of leaves and birds, blending with the voice of a stream which still flowed below ; the stately forest trees, and fruit trees large as forest trees, no doubt festooned with clusters of golden and purple grapes.

The productions of the level base of the little valley were more prosaic, except for their suggestions of home comfort, which give their own peculiar charms to kitchen gardens, and for the beautiful little stream which eddied and prattled along its stony channel. At the head of the valley is an ancient rock-hewn tank, filled with fresh water from a stream which flows into it through the arched entrance of a cool, subterranean chamber. The fountain head is at some little distance, and the water is conveyed into the valley through an ancient excavated aqueduct. From this tank the stream falls in a cascade to the lower level of the valley, by the side of which it flows with the inimitable music of abundant water. The channel is rocky, and overshadowed in many places with steep, wild crags. At the head of the dell, near the tank, some fine old fig trees cast their broad, thick folds of green shade, which is met at its edge by the delicate shadows of pomegranates, then glowing with scarlet blossom. This was quite a bower of shade. Below is a garden of herbs, fruit and vegetables, planted in little spaces, each isolated by its tiny water course. These channels are filled every eight days by the gardener's removing with his foot the little earthen dyke which closes them. It is replaced and the channel cleared in the same way. By this care, two or three crops are obtained in the year. Probably without this Egyptian method (*vide* Deut. xi. 10,) abundant ordinary crops might be procured. These vegetables, herbs, and fruits help to supply the Jerusalem market, as probably, in old times, they supplied Solomon's royal table.

After luncheon and our midday rest we rode to Solomon's magnificent tanks or pools. There are three of these excavated in the solid rock, and in some places supported or approached by walls or steps of massive ancient masonry. They were full on that June afternoon of living water flowing through them.

A ruined castle stood near. But the tanks, which must have been excavated two thousand years at least before a stone of the castle was raised, were not ruined. Throughout the Holy Land no relics of glorious old times are so perfect and so satisfactory as these tanks. Temples, and fortresses, and palaces, are scattered or defaced, but these retain the fresh mark of the workman's tools, and remain a witness—not to the pomp of superstition, or royalty, or war—but to the useful labors of an industrious and prosperous people, and a blessing to the peasants of to-day as to those of three thousand years ago.

Thence we proceeded to Hebron, the city of David's early reign, a rough and hilly ride. It was growing dark before we reached it, and our tired horses stumbled frequently over the rocks and roots on the hillsides. Before night, however, our tents were pitched, and our camp fire was lighted under the shade of "Abraham's oak." The horses, mules and donkeys, with a foal which belonged to one of our mares, and greatly perplexed the riders by its erratic ways, were fastened to stakes near at hand. We commenced mending, sketching, and chatting over adventures, and were at home and at rest as much as pilgrims could wish to be. Vines trailed their luxuriant branches along the ground—stakes to support them being expensive luxuries in this treeless land. The horses were led to water at a neighboring spring; muleteers and servants were grouped in various picturesque attitudes; our dinner was slowly but surely in course of preparation by the Maltese cook; the moonlight fell, chequering the ground through the black massive branches and the delicate leaves of the oak, which was large enough to have sheltered a legion of soldiers. And it was Abraham's oak. Here, on this plain of Mamre, under just such a venerable oak, at the door of a tent (probably more like the camel-hair Bedouin tents than ours) Abraham had welcomed the three mysterious visitors, two of whom were angels. Heavenly feet had trodden this ground. Had heaven grown distant since then, or only invisible, and were such heavenly beings indeed encamping round us for His sake, who in his humiliation needed their ministry once, and commands it always? That God cares for, and protects the feeblest of those who seek his care, we cannot doubt, and He works out his merciful purposes rather with living agents than with unconscious instruments, rather with hands than with machines. Such thoughts often cheered us in our night encampments in the Holy Land, and in regions far more dangerous than Hebron. Although our party happened to be entirely unarmed, I cannot remember experiencing a sensation of fear.

Before breakfast the next morning, June the 18th, we took a beautiful ride along the side of a very fine ravine to Adoraim, the modern Dura. From the top of a mosque near the poor cabins which form the village, we had one of those views so frequent from high land in the centre of Palestine, embracing a large range of hilly country east and

A Mosque.

 p. 164.

west, from the Mediterranean to the hills beyond Jordan, from the sea to the desert.

My horse fell with me at full gallop on some smooth slippery turf, happily just after we had passed the ravine along the precipitous side of which the road wound quite unguarded. I walked back to the tent, and in that way had more leisure to notice the high vineyard walls, built of rough stones, and leaving narrow lanes between them, with occasionally a rude tower at an angle of the walls. These are characteristic of Southern Palestine, and are the lineal descendants of the ancient solitary "cottage in the vineyard." The proprietors often come from their houses in Hebron and live in them during the grape season, at once to enjoy and to protect their property.

In the afternoon we rode to Hebron. It was more like a European town, (not one in England, certainly, but in some remote part of Italy,) than any other place we had seen in Palestine. There were some faint indications of prosperity and life about it; numerous and abundant wells, water troughs, gardens, vineyards, walls not in ruins, reservoirs well kept, even a road in the valley.

We had some slight hope of being permitted to see the inside of the Haram or Sacred Place of Hebron, honored by Moslems, Jews, and Christians as Abraham's Tomb. Mohammedan bigotry had yielded to bribes at Jerusalem, enforced by the echo of our artillery at Sebastopol. And why not here? But all our solicitations were in vain. The authorities of Hebron were either too strictly bound by Mohammedan law, or too ignorant of European politics to pay any attention to our demands. A crowd of angry looking idlers, and boys evidently not averse to the use of physical force, began to collect, and we were obliged to content ourselves with inspecting the outside walls. These were in many parts built of very large stones with that groove round them which we had been told at Jerusalem was characteristic of early Hebrew or Phœnician workmanship, like the stones left in the Temple enclosure. Thus the building carried us back to the days when David dwelt here a king, whilst the cave beneath it is indeed the resting place of Sarah and Leah, Jacob, Isaac, and Abraham, the friend of God.

From Hebron we climbed a steep terraced hill, sometimes scrambling on foot, leading our horses. At the top was a grove of fine old fig trees, reminding one of the groves which crowned the "high places" in ancient days. The view from this was rich and beautiful, and might be taken as some faint likeness of what it must have been in David's time, when the industrious Jews had entered on the olive gardens and vineyards of that earlier race, which, with all its crimes and savage idolatries, must have possessed elements of material civilization lost to the lawless Arab peasants who people the land now. The royal city lay below us, not far off, in the luxuriant plain, from a centre in the valley radiating up three separate hills. Its white roofs, domes, and airy minarets, and especially the great mosque over Machpelah, blended beautifully with the olives, vines and figs which surrounded them. Around was the lovely, rich Plain of Mamre, and beyond, cornfields were still golden on the lower uplands.

Again a night under the shelter of Abraham's oak, and in the morning (Thursday, June 19th) once more across the hill-country of Judea on our way back by Bethlehem to Jerusalem.

The especial interest of this day's journey was that it lay through the heart of the scenery of David's Psalms. The rocks and hill-fortresses, the "thousand hills," and the quiet valleys, the green pastures by the still waters, the wild caves and ravines of the shadow of death, amidst which we journeyed this day, were precisely those which have from our earliest childhood been made allegorical to us by the inspired poetry of the shepherd king.

Our first thoughts, however, in mounting the heights east of the city, were of Abraham's pleading for Sodom on these very hills, and afterwards beholding from the same spot, not the sea of verdure he had seen there before, or the gleam of sunny waters which we see now, but the heavy sea of smoke going up between him and the mountains of Moab,—no wreathed folds of morning mist, but the smoke of a burning land.

The first place we reached was Tekoah, after a wild, rough ride up and down pathless hills. One valley we had much difficulty in crossing. The side was very steep, and clothed or rather thickly sprinkled with trees, the roots of which perplexed our horses, whilst their branches perplexed us, and more than once forcibly recalled the fate of Absalom. At the bottom of this valley, which was a broad level, were corn-fields and meadows, beside an abundant, but still and noiseless stream—"green pastures by still waters," sufficiently rare in this country to impress themselves strongly on the memory. Some peasants were at work in the fields, who warned us off their territories with angry gestures.

Tekoah only differs from the ruined towns or villages which crest almost every hill-top, in its ruins being, although untenanted, more extensive and perfect than usual. This does not imply much; but since "ruins" in the Holy Land frequently mean little more than shapeless heaps of stones, there was a certain interest in exploring the foundations of houses, and the remains of tanks and wells in the city of the "wise woman" of old. The walls of a Greek church were still standing, with large stones of earlier buildings used in its foundations, and a stone font. The chief interest of the place, however, consists in its being one of the "fortresses," the fortified places on the rocky heights of Judea which suggested to David the image so frequent in his Psalms: "Thou," and not these strongholds of my country's hills, "art my refuge and my fortress."

Our next expedition was to the Cave of Adullam, as our guides called it, I suppose incorrectly, since the refuge of David and his outlawed band is considered to have been more probably situated in one of the valleys opening on the rich maritime plains of the Philistines, on whom they made their forays. This mattered little to us—it was doubtless *such* a cave. During the exiled and outlawed period of his life, when David, like so many of whom the world was not worthy, "wandered in deserts and mountains, and in dens and caves of the earth," he had recourse to more than one such hiding-place, and why not to this?

In itself this cave was remarkable, not indeed wrought by stalactite and stalagmite into fairy likenesses of cathedral, palace, or grove, like some of the caves in our own limestone formations, but interesting, nevertheless, from its situation and its size. Its only opening is into a narrow, deep, dry ravine. Its only approach is down a steep mountain-path to a ledge of rock, over which you have to creep on hands and knees, one at a time, round a projecting crag into the cavern. This jutting rock, which effectually screens the entrance, once passed, the opening is large enough to admit abundance of light and air, and introduces you at once into a wide and lofty hall, with a vaulted or dome-shaped roof, the top of which was only lighted up at angles here and there by the daylight, or further in by our torches. This led into other chambers, and into one passage which we did not penetrate. A more secure hiding-glace could scarcely be imagined. The entrance even could not be reached to smoke its tenants out, and except that, no mode of attack, but blockade, could affect them. The opening was about half-way up the perpendicular sides of the ravine. Wild birds flew uneasily about the crags, disturbed by our presence. The deep, narrow glen lay in shade even in that burning mid-day, and suggested forcibly by its lifeless stillness and darkness, in contrast with the valley of still waters and green pastures we had just passed, the other valley mentioned in the same Psalm—the sunless, waterless ravine of the shadow of death.

There was something most interesting in

thus, as it were, approaching the Psalms from the *other side*. Usually the thoughts are present with us, and we illustrate them with David's images. Spiritual life and refreshment—the sure guardianship of our God—his presence lighting us at that hour when all other lights go out,—these are facts familiar to us, and we clothe them in the imagery of stream, and meadow, and dark ravine. But with David, probably this was reversed; he *saw* the still waters, the "cavern hiding-place," the commanding "fortress," the gloomy valley, and he linked these to the realities of the unseen world. Looking at his flocks peacefully feeding under his shepherd care, he thought with happy confidence, "The Lord is *my* shepherd. I would traverse hill and valley before these trusting flocks should lack pasture, and will He suffer me to want?" Or, watchfully leading them through such a desert ravine as this—one of those "desert-creeks," through which Bedouin marauders might invade the peaceful land—without a tuft of herbage or a drop of water to sustain the wearied sheep, gathering the lambs in his arms, carrying the sickly on his shoulders, guarding them and guiding them with his rod and staff, he might feel: "And I also, though I have to pass through a ravine darker and more desolate than this, will fear no evil. These sheep fearlessly follow me here, and I will fearlesly follow thee, my Shepherd; for even there thou shalt be with me. My rod and staff lead and protect them—*Thy* rod and thy staff, they comfort *me*." Or, in after years, looking from this mountain stronghold, or hiding in such a cave as this, he thought, "Not these stone walls and this rocky height, or this inaccessible cavern, are my true security. The Lord is my rock and my fortress, my high tower, my refuge, and my hiding-place."

It is difficult to describe the freshness and beauty which those precious, familiar psalms acquire by being thus visibly approached from the side of the scenery which suggested their imagery.

After leaving "Adullam," or whatever this interesting cave should be called, the next feature of importance in this day's journey was the ascent of the "Frank Mountain." This is a conical hill, with a square, level summit, higher than the hills around, of a peculiar shape among their usual unvaried rounded forms, and commanding a fine view. There are ruins on it, and the mere fact of its having an outline of some character amidst these monotonous heights, is said to have gained it the honor assigned it of being the last fortress held by the crusading Franks in the Holy Land.

Our last point was Bethlehem, to which, on account of the day's journey and the approaching darkness, our visit was unfortunately very hurried.

We lingered a little by the Well of Bethlehem, waiting for some of our party. But, precious as the hours were to us, we could hardly call this time lost, we were so much interested in watching several of the Bethlehem maidens who were drawing water.

Their manners and appearance were so different from most of the peasantry of the country; their bearing was so modest, and yet so frank and trustful; and their movements and figures were so graceful, as they sat on the edge of the well, or helped each other to draw up the heavy pitchers, in their white classical robes, with their head-dresses of gold coins; and their unveiled faces had such a noble beauty, a Greek regularity of feature, combined with such dignity of expression. It seemed as if a glory had fallen on them from the virgin mother of Nazareth, who brought forth here her first-born Son, and wrapped him in swaddling clothes, and laid him in a manger *here.*

I cannot say the refreshment it was to see women once more whose ideas of modesty and good manners consisted in something else than in hiding their faces, and cowering like frightened animals when spoken to. These Bethlehem Christian women are, we were afterwards told, renowned for their beauty and for their good character. They are said to be descendants of the Crusaders. The Europeans of Jerusalem engage them, whenever they can, as upper servants. There was something indescribably touching to me in finding this little knot of free, noble-looking women at the birth-place of Him to whom the women of Christendom owe, in every sense, everything which ennobles and blesses them for eternity and for time.

The water they so courteously drew for us was the water of "the well hard by the gate," which David longed for, but would not drink, as the purchase of the blood of his faithful soldiers—the well to which he had doubtless often repaired when feeding those "few sheep" in the upland pastures near. As we left Bethlehem one of the women we had met at the well, and given some piastres to in acknowledgment of a draught of water, rushed out of a house as we rode by, and took my hand and kissed it fervently. I wonder if that little gift had come at some moment of need, and so awakened that burst of gratitude. It seemed to give one a link with a home at Bethlehem.

Our best views of the town were as we left it, and looked back on it from the hill, the long crest of which its white walls and houses crown,—a brown, bare hill, like the thousand others near, but terraced into vineyards by the Christian population, and looking down on a valley "standing thick with corn," whilst beyond are the pastures of the wilderness where David kept his sheep, and guarded them from the lions and bears which roamed up from the Jordan Valley, and beyond and above again, as always here, the mountain wall of Moab. Cornfields where Ruth gleaned, hills where the boy David kept his sheep; but to us how infinitely more than this—hills where shepherds once kept watch over their flocks by night—where the glory of the Lord shone round them through the midnight—where the voices of a great multitude of the heavenly host sang, "Glory to God in the highest"—where the Lord of angels, higher than heaven, once lay, a babe wrapped in swaddling-clothes, cradled in a manger. "For unto *us* was born that day in the city of David a Saviour, which is Christ the Lord."

I have often since thought it was unwise, but then and there our hearts revolted from the beads, and relics, and even the Church of the Nativity, with its candles, and silver shrines, and marble floors. Cannot any one see it any day at a diorama in London? At all events, we did not visit it. I know that the subsequent historical interest of that church is great—that it was one of the earliest sanctuaries of Christendom—that Jerome, the fervent, stern, rugged father, lived there in a cave for years. But I cannot, on the whole, regret that our unmixed associations with Bethlehem were of frank and noble-looking Christian women drawing water for us from David's well; of a white town cresting a hill where shepherds feed their flocks, and at whose foot rest golden corn-fields, and where all subsequent historical events are merged in the one event which began all

Christian history—that He to whom every knee in heaven and earth shall bow once lay there, a babe, on a poor Galilean woman's breast, He who on the throne of heaven wears that nature still.

We returned to Jerusalem by the Hill of Evil Counsel, with its one solitary tree, passing in an hour or two from the mountain village where we know the Saviour was born to the desolate fields where it is said the traitor died.

Once more, and for the last time, we returned to Jerusalem as our home, and felt how even the most interesting and sacred minor associations of this wonderful land are dim and distant compared with the thoughts which gather round every minutest touch and incident of that one life and death which are to us, in the midst of all the darkness of earth and time, light and life, wisdom and redemption, the opening of heaven, and the manifestation of God.

IX.

Church of the Holy Sepulchre,

AND THE

LAST VIEW OF JERUSALEM.

WE had left our visit to the Church of the Holy Sepulchre until our last day in Jerusalem, not purposely, but because localities more satisfactorily ascertained, and less desecrated by superstition, had engrossed our attention.

There are three distinct sets of historic association which give interest to this land of ruins ; the events of the old Jewish history, of the sixty years during which the New Testament was lived and written, and the Crusades, that great revulsion of European life to the East.

With the first of these periods the Church

of the Holy Sepulchre has, of course, nothing to do. With the second, it has (at least in the opinion of many) but a very doubtful connection. One verse in one Gospel might have set at rest for ever, in a few words, the question of the situation of Calvary, and therefore of the Sepulchre. No such verse exists, and in the absence of direct proof, one can only hope that the place which is annually desecrated by an imposture and a fight amongst those who bear the name of Christ, is *not* Calvary.

But with the third period, the era of the Crusades, or rather the whole of the middle ages, the Church of the Holy Sepulchre is the great central point, the inmost sanctuary and shrine of mediæval faith, the sacred relic around which the battle of Moslem and Christian raged for centuries.

In visiting this Church, we felt as if we were leaving the home of Jewish kings and prophets, and the earthly footprints of the Son of God, to enter on a region full, indeed, of deep human and historical interest, but altogether on a lower level, more of an interest akin to that which we feel in Rome or Canterbury, although in an intenser degree.

Our thought, as we descended the steps into the court outside the Church, was not so much of Golgotha, or the tomb hewn in the rock, as of the countless pilgrim feet which had trodden those steps for centuries, of the innumerable hearts which had throbbed with eager joy, or almost stood still with awe in approaching those sacred walls.

The front and the arched doors are very massive and elaborately ornamented. You compare them mentally, not with anything in the Bible, but with Venice, or Milan, or Cologne. You are transported into the middle ages, the middle ages orientalized. You pass from the burning sacrifice into the dark church. You are no longer in the city where David dwelt—where Nicodemus came to Jesus by night—by which the brook Kedron flowed—to which her King came, lowly and riding on an ass—and which the little children entered, singing Hosannahs in the light of the spring morning—where the blind and lame were touched by those healing hands, and walked and saw. You are in another world, lighted, not by the blaze of the Syrian sun, or by the starlight of the Syrian night, but by faint rays stealing through mediæval windows. The air around you is no breeze from the Great Sea, or the mountains beyond Jordan, but the air of a vault perfumed with incense.

The group of Moslem soldiers sitting on a raised matted stone platform at the left of the entrance, reminds you for an instant of the scenes enacted here at Easter, when Turkish sabres have to restrain Christian worshippers from tearing each other in pieces in their eagerness to light their torches at the "sacred fire," a singular collision of three religions, Mohammedan, Christian, and Pagan. But passing on, you forget this strange discord, and are back again in the days of Richard Cœur de Lion, or of Godfrey of Bouillon, and then mediæval religion seems to rise before you allegorized in stone.

The Church of the middle ages is indeed the Church of the Holy Sepulchre. Although there can be no doubt that throughout the middle ages there was always a Church of the living Saviour, it is a most significant fact that the centre of Christendom in those days was a tomb. A sacred tomb indeed, but yet with reverence be it spoken, a tomb not sacred even as that of Stephen or Paul would have been, for it was an empty tomb.

The grave of the humblest Christian contains relics which one day are to be quickened into glorious, incorruptible beauty. The sepulchre of Christ, could it have been found, would have contained nothing but the stone ledge, " the place where the Lord lay." The dust of the grave clothes might be there ; the angels had gone back to heaven or were ministering to some lowly Hagar or little child on earth ; the embalming spices had never been needed there. May we not feel that the lowliest sod beneath which the dust of a Christian lies, and over which the eyes of Christ watch to awake it into immortality, is more truly sacred than that empty sepulchre? May we not be sure that the body in which the Holy Spirit dwelt, and which shall awake in the likeness of the Lord, is more truly a relic of our Redeemer, than the abandoned grave clothes and the empty tomb? Yet it was by this empty sepulchre that mediæval Christendom stood without, like the Magdalene, weeping. The best and most characteristic of its hymns are tinged with deep melancholy. Their fragrance is that of the embalming spices, rather than of the resurrection morning. Their gaze is into the darkness of the sepulchre, instead of towards the light into the face of the risen Saviour.

Surely those pilgrimages to the Holy Sepulchre are as contrary to the whole spirit of Christianity, as the worship of the glorified Virgin Mother—"Mary the Immaculate." which has succeeded them. To turn from the living Lord to the abandoned tomb is as strange a perversion as to turn from the dying Redeemer on the cross to the mournful mother beside it,—

> " 'Tis life whereof our nerves are scant,
> Oh life, not death, for which we pant—
> More life and fuller that we want."

And ours is a religion of life; our Lord the Prince of life, the Bread of Life, the Life itself, who burst the bands of death, because it was not possible that he should be holden of them. All this presses sensibly on the heart in the Church of the Holy Sepulchre. It is the religion of the Crusades petrified, and the spirit of the middle ages comes over you as you stand within these massive walls.

The wretched rivalries of the various Churches, and the "narrowing lust of gold" which fosters these rivalries, are on a lower level again. But these did not build the grand arches, or heap every sacred spot with precious stones and metals. It was a true devotion which is represented here, however below the truth may be its objects.

That flight of steps leading to a stone platform, which to you may seem little more than the rood-loft, or the Calvary of any mediæval church, is what Crusaders died to win. Countless forms have been prostrated there in passionate adoration. We saw a man reverently embracing and kissing column after column. As you stand there the thought comes overpoweringly to you, "Can this indeed be Calvary? the place where the Cross stood, the three crosses? Did our Saviour's dying eyes indeed look down from this height on the sea of curious and mocking faces of those who had come to see that sight, and on the three women and one apostle who ventured to stand close beside Him, before that angry crowd, and confess that they loved Him? If so, you feel that in order to feel any realization of the scene, you must shut your eyes and exclude all the incongruous treasures with which the industrious devotion of centuries has encumbered the place. If this once irregular hillock were indeed Golgotha, and the new sepulchre wherein never yet man lay, beside which the voice of the risen Saviour was first heard, was indeed where that shrine now stands, then what a desecration this building is! What one would give to be able to sweep away this heavy roof, and this wretched gold, and these marbles, and look up from this very spot to the sky which was veiled at midday, and over the guilty city which had poured out her multitudes to witness, without a remonstrance the perpetration of that unequalled crime! We guard with jealous care every trace of our national heroes or our beloved dead,—the pen laid down as it was left, the poor chairs and table where Luther and his Catherine sat, the unfinished work, the garden walk "where prayer was wont to be made." Why, then, can Christendom have combined to destroy every thing which was characteristic in this place of most sacred memories to us all?

The only thought which enables one at all to comprehend it, is that in the Empress Helena's time, when the "Invention of the Holy Cross" took place, the memory of the cross as an infamous punishment had not passed away from the world. Golgotha was a place of ignominy, and we can easily imagine the devotion of the Christian empress leading her to bury every trace of her Saviour's rejection beneath all that the imperial treasuries could offer of costly magnificence. Well as one can comprehend such a feeling, how far more precious to us would have been the broken ground, the bare, roughly hewn rock, the open view of Olivet, Jerusalem, and the sky.

The Holy Sepulchre itself is one mass of gold and silver, and precious marbles, seen by the dim light of silver lamps.

There are some less ornamental tombs—one called Joseph's—in a vault belonging to the Copts. Latins, Greeks, Copts, Armenians, Syrians, all have a corner in the sacred edifice. The various Churches seem to have taxed their ingenuity to find sacred names and events to consecrate their several territories, and to secure some especial attraction for their especial votaries. We are sinking into a region below that of religious sentimentalism, or even of ecclesiastical controversy, to the lowest deep of petty mercenary competitions. In every sense it is a relief to escape from the dim church, with its heavy atmosphere, into the daylight and the fresh air.

For ours is indeed a religion of life, not of sepulchres or relics. Our sanctuaries are not the twilight of umbrageous groves, or the night of oracular caverns or monumental vaults. Precious, indeed, is every relic of the work of the hand we may touch no more, but the hand of Him we adore is working around us everywhere. Every star which shines, and every blossom that opens is not a relic of His absent work, but a token of His living presence. The voice which said, "It is finished," is not silenced for us. We know it. It speaks to us day by day in ever loving words. The true reliquary of the Church of Christ is the Bible. Let us treasure, if we will, every relic of the dead we honor. But Christ is not dead. He is risen. He was dead and is living again, and behold he liveth for evermore.

There is, indeed, a sense in which we on earth are said to be absent from the Lord, but never is it said that the Lord is absent from us. On the contrary, He is with us always until the end of the world. Death removes us to be present with Him. Resurrection gathers together the whole Church to be for ever with Him, consciously, visibly, eternally. But now to day, and "all the days," He is with us. He makes His abode with us. He will never leave us nor forsake us.

Have not all representations of the church as a "widow," or a "widowed bride," a tendency to sentimentalism? The Bible never uses this language. The image employed in Epistles and Apocalypse is one of an entirely different character. The widow is desolate, lonely, her gaze is towards the past, to the life finished and closed. The heart of the betrothed bride is in the future, in the day which ends separation, in the new life opening before her. The Bible compares the Church, not to the widow, but to the betrothed bride. The marriage supper has yet to take place. The new and everlasting home is being prepared; it has yet to be entered. The attitude of all healthy Christianity is not stooping down and looking into the sepulchre weeping, "They have taken away my Lord," but looking up to the risen Lord, and listening to his voice, and answering, Rabboni.

We left the church and ascended the steps worn by the feet or knees of so many pilgrims, and descended the Via Dolorosa with its "*window* of the Ecce Homo," and its various legendary stations.

What a strange reversal of the parables the Crusades were — a Pilgrim's progress read the wrong way; the body making a pilgrimage to a material Jerusalem; the Christian armor, mail or steel, instead of faith, and the word of God, and prayer; the Christian warfare against the bodies of Moslems instead of against fleshly lusts and wicked spirits. If the Crusades had only been an allegoric drama enacted for the benefit of posterity, they certainly might be valued as tending to give vividness to our conceptions of the true warfare of the Cross. But the Crusaders were men and women with human hearts and deathless souls. Among them must have been some who really longed, like Christian, to get rid of that terrible burden, who travelled all that perilous journey with the fond hope that at the Holy Sepulchre they would in some way be nearer heaven, would obtain spiritual deliverance, and receive spiritual blessing. To such, what agonizing conflict and bitter disappointment must have been spent here, when the first rush of enthusiastic devotion had subsided! The burden of guilt unremoved, the power of sin unbroken, heaven as far as ever, the Saviour as invisible! Yet, perchance, on many such, as they turned their steps despondingly homeward, the glad tidings dawned that the crucified and risen Lord could be as near them in Germany or England as at Jerusalem, and that the Holy War, so often a defeat in Palestine, might in his strength be always victorious in works of faith and labors of love at home.

We returned from the Church of Helena and the Crusaders to the Turkish city of to-day. Everywhere we were surrounded by tokens which showed how the great conflict of the middle ages had ended. Moslem shopkeepers sat composedly smoking in the bazaars; Moslem women passed us with their veiled faces; Moslem domes crowned the heights of Moriah; Moslem muezzins called to prayer from the galleries of the minarets. The very name of Christian is a bond. We must lament that the curse of Moslem rule should fall on any spot on earth. Yet we cannot but feel that as regards the sacred association of the Holy Land, Moslem listlessness, and even Moslem fanaticism, have done less to destroy them than monastic superstitions. Two or three centuries of Crusading rule would have left little but a mass of mediæval legends to guide us through Palestine. Turkish rule has, at least, left it Oriental. The language of the peasantry is still allied to that in which our Lord awoke the dead maiden to life, and uttered his own cry of agony. The names of villages, and fountains, and towns are still essentially the same as those in the Old Testament. The traditions of monks who would find you the locale of any spiritual narrative (whether parable or history) within convenient distances of each other, on sufficient notice, are valueless indeed. But the traditions of peasants who have never read the Old or New Testament, and yet spake of Shiloh, or Nazareth, or Tyre, by names David could have understood, are absolutely satisfactory. Our wonder in the Holy Land was, not that we could trace so little, but that we could identify so much. Once leave the narrow streets and Saracenic gates of the city itself, and you are on the very hills and valleys where Jesus "went about doing good." Deeply did we feel this, as on the afternoon of the twentieth of June, we at length collected our muleteers and horses, and set off two or three hours before night for Bethel. The hills which stand round about Jerusalem were real and familiar places to us for evermore.

We had toiled through the stony bottom of the dark valley of Hinnom. We had sat one sunny Sunday afternoon on the Hill of Evil Counsel, looking across the valley to the slopes of Zion. We had gone round about the walls of Jerusalem, commanding from different angles the table-land on the west, the deep valleys on the east and south. We had drunk of the clear, cold waters which flow underneath the temple. We had stood by the ancient reservoirs, one of which must have been Bethesda, and another the Pool of Siloam, for since Roman times no energetic and enlightened rule has continued long enough to commence useful public works of any such extent as these. We had groped our way through the rifled sepulchres, whose entrances no one, for centuries, had cared to "whiten" or adorn. We had carefully guided our horses over the rough ground outside the gates, and among the broken cisterns and deserted wells, which made such dangerous "pits" for them to fall into. We had rambled over the slopes of Zion, and gathered the long dagger-like thorns which grow on the prickly bushes there. We had explored the Temple area, and stood on the very place where the blind eyes had first seen, and lame feet had first walked, and the deaf ears had been unstopped at the touch or word of Jesus;—where, in the women's court, that all might approach and learn, our Lord taught openly, and even as he spoke words of eternal wisdom, and answered every subtle cavil, was at leisure to watch and mark with his approval the poor widow casting her mites into the treasury.

We had crossed the brook Kedron, and wandered up the valley, in some quiet nook of which, among the olives, was Gethsemane. We had watched from Olivet the sunrise light up the roofs of Jerusalem, and the sunset glow behind them. We had seen the city over which, when He beheld

Bethany.

it, He wept, burst suddenly on our sight, in that ascent on the road from Jericho. We had sat on the Mount of Olives, and gazed across the Kedron valley to where the goodly buildings had stood, now overthrown. We had gone over and over again the footpath to Bethany, with the wild fig-trees beside it here and there, until its rugged way had grown familiar to us. Seated on those very slopes under the shade of trees, more abundant no doubt than now, treading those very paths, sheltered in the recesses of that same valley, the voice of Jesus had been heard in familiar conversation with the disciples. On that same level summit of Moriah, His voice, in more powerful tones, had taught the listening multitudes, and silenced the cavilling Pharisees and Sadducees, not with the majesty of thunder, or the voice as of a trumpet, or as the sound of many waters, but a human voice, whose tones would have been inaudible at a few hundred yards distance,—a human voice, thrilling with every emotion of the heart.

The words have gone forth to the ends of the earth, the voice would have been inaudible across the Kedron valley.

Within sight of those walls near the city, the three crosses had been raised with the three agonized sufferers on them, exposed to the unpitying gaze of the multitudes who came to see the sight, and the careless mockeries of those that passed by on the high road from Jerusalem. The mystical shadow of one of those crosses has since then embraced the world, and within it a great multitude, which no man can number— have found shelter, and safety, and rest. But then, before the midday darkness came over the land, there was nothing to distinguish it from the other two, or from the number of similar crosses which afterwards terribly exposed the agonies of their victims to the gaze of besieged Jerusalem. There was nothing gigantic about it, infinite as its results will be. It overshadowed, not the city, but only a few yards of earth beneath it, and at a little distance you would not have distinguished one of those three tortured forms from another, infinitely different as the sufferers were,—the Saviour, the saved, and the lost.

And on these heights of Olivet, above Bethany, that human voice had been heard again, in familiar tones, blessing the disciples. The hands that had been stretched out and nailed to the cross were lifted up to bless. And there, in the act of benediction, the well-known form was parted from them, and carried into heaven, mastering all planetary laws with divine majesty, yet, like another human body, lessening to the upturned gaze of the disciples in the distance above them, until the intervening cloud hid Him from their sight.

It was this truth of the humanity of our Lord which so often came on us with startling distinctness in these pathways He had trodden, that He was actually a man. Our dim and imperfect thoughts vibrate so easily from one mistake to another, in endeavoring to realize his twofold nature, unconsciously mystifying His humanity into something super-human, illimitable, half divine, or humanizing His Deity. Yet in the perfect distinctness of the two natures is the glory of their perfect union, and on it depends much of our practical comfort and strength,—

> Perfect God and perfect man: of a reasonable soul and human flesh subsisting,
> Equal to the Father as touching His godhead: and inferior to the Father as touching His manhood.
> Who although He be God and man; yet he is not two, but one Christ,—
> One, not by conversion of the Godhead into flesh, but by taking of the manhood unto God.
> One altogether, not by confusion of substance, but by unity of person.

It was with thoughts such as these that we rode silently away from Jerusalem on the afternoon of the 20th of June. Our road lay across Scopas, and the site of the camp of Titus. On this ground the armies of Rome had encamped, slowly but surely clasping the infatuated city in their deadly embrace, and here those who may have been left to guard the camp in the day of the capture, must have seen the avenging flames burst forth from the temple on Moriah, no more as from a sacrificial altar, but as from the funeral pile of the guilty city, from which every single disciple of the Saviour it had crucified had previously been rescued.

Once more on the height to the north (to which Mr. Nicolayson had guided us in our first ride, as presenting the finest view of Jernsalem), we paused to take our last view of it. The only human feature in the desolate landscape, the city rests couched on the edge of the high table-land of Judæa; the mural crown enclasps the brow of the hill, the white roofs, the domes, and minarets gleam from afar, still with something of a queenly dignity. The brown hills stand round about it, the blue mountains of Moab gird the distant horizon. Beautiful for situation it stands, the mountain city, the city where David dwelt, the holy city, the city which God chose, the city over which "Jesus wept," desecrated by man's darkest crime, consecrated by the most marvellous manifestation of God's redeeming love.

X.

Bethel, Shiloh,

AND THE WELL AT SYCHAR.

THE daylight which had served us for our last view of Jerusalem began to decline soon after we turned northward from that point, and descended the hills which hid from us the holy city and the hill-country of Judea.

It is seldom possible to start on a long expedition in the East early in the day. Our departure had been delayed by a stormy debate in the courtyard of Simeon's hotel, between the dragoman and the muleteers. The Arab muleteers had endeavored to persuade us to take two or three inferior horses, and on a journey which was to last a month this was a point which could not be yielded, and the English consul for Caiapha and the French consul kindly came to our aid.

We felt sure the contest would end as we wished, and meantime could do nothing but watch the progress of the debate and regret the loss of time. Voices were raised to angry shrieks and lowered to fierce menacing murmurs; the faces of the disputants expressed the most violent passions. The dark eyes glared and flashed, and the lips of some foamed with rage, and hands were raised in deprecatory or threatening gesticulation. The muleteers began to detach the trunks, and seemed on the point of leading away their animals and abandoning the bargain. Our dragoman helplessly stormed and pleaded; the English consul stood calm amidst the tempest, occasionally throwing in a few strong words which at first increased the clamor, but finally calmed it. The whole was to us like a most vivid drama or pantomime, the gestures and expression of the disputants rendering the knowledge of the language scarcely necessary to the comprehension of their meaning.

At length the horses we declined were led away, the horses we wanted were brought in their stead, and our whole caravan clattered out of the court-yard and over the rough stony streets. But the loss of time in this debate had left us only one hour's daylight for the four hours' journey to Bethel, where our tents were to be pitched for the night.

After we turned from our last lingering gaze at Jerusalem the sun sank behind the western hills, and almost before we had begun to think of the decline of the day the brief twilight was over, and it was dark.

The guide, who rode before us, was deaf to all our entreaties to relax his pace. We scrambled on after him in the dark over the rough roads. The darkness deepened; no moon rose, and the stars which glittered so brilliantly above us, and the fireflies which darted to and fro on each side or across our path, only made the blackness of the night more apparent. To attempt to guide the horses was in vain; nothing was visible but the ghostly apparition of a white horse before me, of which I must on no account lose sight. Up and down the stony path we scrambled, but might have been quite tranquil if we could have trusted our safe agile little Syrian horses as they deserved. They never made a false step; but we were not sorry to find our tents pitched at Bireh (Beeroth), when we reached it, instead of having to ride an hour further to Bethel, our original destination.

We had to rise very early on the following morning. A long day's journey was before us to Nablous (Shechem), and the lost hour of the preceeding day had to be made up.

The way between Beeroth and Bethel lay over craggy hills, reminding us again of Dartmoor, only brown and grassless, and of limestone instead of granite. On the height of Bethel are the ruins of a Greek church and several old foundations of houses with large stones. Beyond these was a rocky hil' strewn with many rough stones, of which Jacob might have made a pillow, or afterwards Jeroboam altar-stones for his rival temple.

And this is Bethel, "the house of God," where in vision the angel's ladder rested, linking Jacob's pillow to the throne of God. What made it "dreadful" and sublime? Certainly not any intrinsic beauty or sublimity in the scenery. When Jacob lighted on it it was "a certain place." No more characteristic word is found to describe it. He rested there, not because it was a place of streams or groves, or shady rocks, or in any way a tempting shelter, but just for the same reason we had tarried at Beeroth, "because the sun was set." It was a place in itself no more attractive or sublime than Jacob's own very ordinary character. It was no snowy Alpine summit, forming naturally a flight of spotless altar-steps from earth to heaven—a pedestal on which one could well imagine the angelic ladder might have rested. It was an ordinary brown hill-side strewn with rough stones, over which passed the high road. Nor was it fenced off from common ground, like Moriah, by precipitous ravines. You could not define the moment when you arrived at it or left it. There was nothing to distinguish it from any of the undulations or hills around.

When Jacob laid down to sleep, it was to him a bare featureless hillside strewn with stones, which he could not have recognized when he returned from Haran among the many similar places around. When he awoke out of sleep he said, "Surely the Lord is in this place, and I knew it not." There was no terror, or majesty, or beauty inherent in the place, especially to reveal or symbolize the divine presence. But God was there. This was its consecration and its glory. Heaven had been opened to Jacob's vision there. The voice of the Lord had spoken to his spirit there in human words, and therefore the place was full of solemnity and majesty to him. It was the house of God. And then when he returned, a patriarch and a prosperous man from his long exile, he built an altar and called the place El Bethel, because there God appeared unto him,—an altar of the religion whose highest manifestation is not in nature, or sun or stars, or mountains, but in the Son of man.

The subsequent history of Bethel has little more religious interest for us than that of any heathen shrine—a scene of idolatrous worship, with the old Egyptian animal symbols recalled by Jeroboam from Egypt, of feasts and sacrifices mocking and parodying God's ordinances at Jerusalem, of prophetic denunciation, and at last of judgment, when the bones of false priests and prophets were exhumed from the tombs among these hills, and burnt and strewn to the winds on an altar formed of these shattered stones.

Temple, city, altar, shady grove, all the relics of that idolatrous ritual have perished without a trace, and the bare hill-sides lie again ordinary and stony, and solitary and dreary, as when sunset surprised Jacob upon it, and the heavenly vision transformed the place in his eyes from a sweep of barren moorland into a gate of heaven.

From Bethel we rode along a rough water-course, through a richly wooded valley among figs, olives and vines, to a dell where was an ancient well. From this we crossed a plain to the foot of a steep hill crowned by a village, called by our guides Sinjel. Its situation was more picturesque than usual. The height on which it stood was rocky and precipitous, with an abundant ice-cold spring in the centre of the poor rough cabins, rising under the shadow of an arch, rudely hewn in the rock. We dismounted at the well, and some of the women filled their pitchers from the deep spring, and poured water into the stone troughs for our horses and then gave us to drink, women and children flocking round us, and curiously examining our Frank dresses and faces while we rested. This fine spring is probably the cause why this village is still inhabited, among the numbers of deserted towns and villages which are dotted over the hills and valleys of this old inheritance of Benjamin. We led our horses down the precipitous rocky path from Sinjel to the plain, and after a short gallop across the level, reached another village on the plain, which the dragoman called Turmus Ayeh. The scriptural names I do not know, and yet, probably, there is not a village we pass but dates back to early Hebrew times, if not beyond these to the days of the Hittite and the Perizzite, with their gigantic stones, and cities walled up to heaven. Everywhere when you come amongst human dwellings in this country, you find traces of more energetic races, large regularly squared stones, tanks hewn in the rock for rain-water; broken cisterns once cemented and lined with stone, now holding no water; threshing-floors, levelled on the rocky hill-sides, where the wind would act as a natural "fan," sweeping the chaff from the grain; wells with stone seats on their edge; fine old terraces, for vines and olives, broken in many places and bared by the winter torrents. Everywhere traces of industrious and skilful men, yet no ruins, only heaps of stones, squared and chiseled carefully, it may be, but scattered, except here and there the remains of a church built by the Crusaders, patched and twisted into a mosque. The wheels of time, and conquest, and misgovernment have ground too heavily over the land, to leave anything of value above the surface. It is only the *Intaglio* relics that are left perfect; the traces of labor graven in on the solid rock in tanks, and threshing-floors, and terraces cut out of the hill-sides.

Our next point of interest was Shiloh. Its name on the lips of the ignorant peasantry, unperplexed by any monastic tradition, identifies it. It is called Seilun. An ancient well marks the place where Shiloh was, and the hillside is thickly strewn with stones, interspersed with tufts of parched vegetation. It is, indeed, a desolation, a desolation of many generations. Nowhere do Bible words come more vividly to the mind than here.

Here the ark found its first resting place after the wanderings in the wilderness were over. Here the yearly feast was held to the Lord, when the daughters of Shiloh came out to dance in the dances. To this dreary, solitary spot, untenanted even by Arab peasants, with its dry well on the stony hill, the tribes of Israel came up of old to worship from the maritime plains and the west, through the eastern passes, from the first settlements in wooded Gilead and the Jordan valley, from the hills of Judæa on the south.

Here too, is the undoubted locality of that touching story which, almost earlier than any other, is listened to by little children in Christian lands. On this very spot the infant Samuel heard God speak. The scene of the dear old nursery picture we all know is actually here. Here Hannah came year after year to the sacrifice in bitterness of soul. Here one year, rising from the feast where none but Elkanah would miss her presence, she knelt outside the curtained Tabernacle, on this hillside, beneath this clear azure sky. And on one of these stones, scattered around us, then a seat, Eli sat and watched the speechless, quivering lips, and marked that woman of a sorrowful spirit in the agony of her voiceless prayers, and unlike the High Priest in the holiest now for evermore, misunderstood the broken-hearted suppliant, and reproached her as if the cup which so overflowed for her had been a cup of intoxication instead of one of reproach and grief. And up this hill she came again with her little son, and dedicated him to God, no more speechless and sad, her gratitude overflowing in a song whose prophetic words blend with that other song, also from a woman's lips, that magnificat in which all Christendom shares, singing evermore, "To us a child is born, a Son is given."

And to this sanctuary, year after year, she came up again. The feet of her children tripping up this hillside beside her, their prattling voices in her ears and blending them with hers in thanksgiving, as she brought that annual gift to her firstborn, and clothed him in the little coat her hands had been busy with before she came.

And here, not on the open hill, but in the tented temple, the child Samuel ministered to the Lord, and one night, in the dim lamp-light, as he lay down to sleep near the ark, heard that mysterious voice, three times repeated, and at last understood, and answered by the childish voice in the words we know so well, "Speak, Lord, for thy servant heareth."

Then came the doom of the house of Eli, and the old man, once more sitting on a seat by the wayside (as when before he had marked Hannah) received the terrible tidings of the ruin of his house, and of his people, and when he heard of the capture of the sacred ark, fell backward from his seat and died—on this hillside.

Thus the ark and the divine presence passed from Shiloh, and the name of Shiloh passes from the Bible. The dominion of Benjamin, Ephraim, and Manasseh is transferred to Judah. The sanctuary is transferred to Zion. Then, after the lapse of centuries, the name of Shiloh is heard again from the lips of the prophet of lamentation (Jer. vii. 12—14; xxvi. 8). It had passed into a by-word of desolation and ruin. "But go ye now unto my place which was in Shiloh, where I set my name at the first, and see what I did to it for the wickedness of my people Israel. And now, because ye have done all these works, saith the Lord, and I spake unto you, rising up early and speaking, but ye heard not; and I called you, but ye answered not; therefore will I do unto this house, which is called by my name, wherein ye trust, and unto the place which I gave to you and to your fathers, as I have done to Shiloh."

The prophecy evidently made a deep impression, for "Now it came to pass, when Jeremiah had made an end of speaking all that the Lord commanded him to speak unto all the people, that the priests, and the prophets, and all the people, took him, saying, Thou shalt surely die. Why hast thou prophesied in the name of the Lord, saying, This house shall be like Shiloh, and this city shall be desolate without an inhabitant? And all the people were gathered against Jeremiah in the house of the Lord."

Through the crimes of the later monarchy this desolate hill stood a warning to Jerusalem. To us who had stood so lately on the site of the leveled temple of Jerusalem, and had thus seen both desolations accomplished, the ruin which the Jews of Jeremiah's time knew so well, and the ruin which they thought so impossible, this dreary hill of Seilun had indeed a solemn interest, rare even in this land of promise and of doom.

We turned away from the scene of so many tender and terrible memories, where human hearts had throbbed with such varied passions of grief, and joy, and despair, and resumed our journey.

On the side of a hill near Shiloh we saw the cavities of many tombs. On another height near it we explored two considerable, but not very ancient ruins, of an Egyptian-looking church, supported by pyramidal buttresses, with a few olives near it, and three broken Corinthian columns prostrate inside, and of a mosque, shaded by a beautiful evergreen oak.

Our visit to Shiloh had taken us out of the main route; for Shiloh (Judges xxi. 19) is on the north side of Bethel, on the east side of the highway that goeth up from Bethel to Shechem, and on the south of Lebonah.

From Bethel we came; we had turned to the east out of the highway to see Shiloh, and now we resumed the caravan route at Lebonah (El Lubban) on our way to Shechem (Nablous).

Near El Lubban we made our midday halt in a valley under the shade of olives, and refreshed ourselves with oranges and hard eggs —the contents of our saddle bags. Here a disappointment befell us, which certainly gave us a strong practical illustration of the value of water in these lands. We had sent the German servant, Wilhelm, to a well a mile off for water, and after waiting for some time, had the satisfaction of seeing him galloping up to us with the water-skin trickling at every step, so that, when he reached us, it only contained a wine-glass full. In a small way we could understand what the Israelites felt at Marah. But there was no resource. We had too long a journey before us to risk fatiguing the horses with any further expeditions, and the precious drops were generously declined by all, and at last conscientiously divided among all, and mixed with wine—at that moment by far the least valued beverage of the two. That, however, and oranges consoled us ; and in an hour or two we remounted and went on our way over one rocky hill after another, with occasionally a white village cresting some height in the distance, or a grove of olives dotting the hillsides, until on the summit of one of the hills, we caught a glimpse, far off, of a tower which we were told was on a height above Nablous. Between us and it rose other lower hills, and a plain or broad valley in which the brown earth was chequered by a mosaic of that greenest green of young corn. In this valley was " the parcel of ground which Jacob gave to his son Joseph."

In descending from the brow of this hill we again lost sight of our landmark and of the plain. In the side of the hill the path wound by a well deep in the shade of a rocky arch. We were too thirsty to consider what the character of the water might be, and eagerly filled our water bottles to drink. But the water was green and very objectionable. A little further on, at the commencement of the plain near Nablous, we met a shepherd boy with a flock of sheep and goats. We asked him for some of the milk of the flock, and he milked some of the goats for us and gave us a draught. I would recommend no one to try this remedy. The new milk certainly increased our thirst, and in a very short time made our throats and lips feel more parched and dry than ever.

But while we were waiting for our beverage we had leisure to consider the scene. We were probably just in the district where Joseph, the shepherd boy, went to see if it was well with the shepherds, his brethren, and well with their flocks. "Jacob sent him out of the vale of Hebron, and he came to Shechem, and a certain man found him wandering in the field."

These fields, just such flocks as these, and Joseph a shepherd boy, with probably just such a dress as the lad who gave us the milk to drink,—a short tunic, with a wrap like a plaid, over his shoulders, and a crook,—a boy with a clear, brown skin, and a lithe, agile figure. He recalled vividly to us the shepherd prince's son, except that Joseph was clothed in the coat of many colors, the coat which was afterwards dipped in the blood of a kid, and taken to bear its false tale of death to the father who gave it.

We turned away with some reluctance from our suggestive shepherd lad, with his quiet white sheep and black goats browsing around him, and rode along the hillside towards the entrance of the valley of Shechem. The valley became very rich, in some places green with young corn, which we believed to be maize, and in others golden with wheat-fields ripe already to the harvest.

Two bandit-like Bashi-Bazouks joined us here, and gave us a specimen of their ingenuity as horsemen, and their regard for the property of the people they profess to protect, by galloping their swift Arab horses through the corn-fields, wheeling round and round among the ripe grain, and ruthlessly trampling it down. We remonstrated in vain through our dragoman. They evidently stood as much in need as any of their predecessors in this oppressed land of the lessons of John the Baptist.

Towards evening we reached the entrance of the valley of Nablous, one of the few places in Palestine which has preserved the intrusive Greek name (Neapolis) instead of the earlier scriptural one, Shechem or Sychar. The narrower valley of Shechem branches off from the broad valley we had been skirting, to the left, between the mountains Ebal and Gerizim.

It is said that no place in Palestine is more absolutely identified as connected with an event in the history of our Lord than this spot. And this spot at the meeting of the valleys, links together the sacred history of more than three thousand years.

Here is Jacob's well, dug by the prudent patriarch, (whose father, Isaac, had had so many disputes about wells), in the parcel of ground he bought from Hamor, and, perhaps, at once given to Joseph, then the only son of Rachel. Here the children of Israel laid the body of Joseph, which they had brought embalmed from Egypt. Here one of the most dramatic scenes in Jewish history was enacted, when the whole multitudes of victorious Israel, with the strangers among them, the women and the children, stood in two great companies, covering these two hills, and probably the valley between and around them, whilst Joshua read the blessings and the curses of the law successively from Ebal and Gerizim, and, from time to time, the deep Amen of the nation echoed from height to height, and swept through the plain. And here Jesus, with all these recollections speaking to him from hill and valley, "being wearied with the journey, sate thus on the well." And to us all the other memories of the plain shine through the light of the last.

We turned off a little to the right to see this sacred spot, but a very great disappointment awaited us. Until last January, they told us, the well had been preserved—a relic of three thousand years, and of one hour worth them all! Until last January you could sit on the edge of the well, and look down into the depths too deep for Him to draw from. But this year the Arabs had broken and scattered the stones, and filled the well with rubbish. The Christians and Turks had been at war in Nablous, a Turk had been accidentally killed by a Christian; and they told us the filling of this well was an act of revenge on the part of the Moslems, knowing how sacred it was to Christians. It made us feel very bitterly, as we stood among the scattered stones and heaps of rubbish where the well had been.

Near this melancholy ruin is the tomb

called Joseph's. It is a holy place of the Moslems, plastered and domed like the tombs of Mohammedan saints. But there is one interesting feature about it in connection with Jacob's blessing to Joseph, comparing him to the "fruitful bough by a well whose branches run over the wall." A fine old vine springs out of the tomb throwing its green leaves and fruitful branches over the wall.

As we rode to and from this tomb some peasants, working in the fields, warned us away from the place with furious gestures, but whether they thought our own infidel feet would desecrate Joseph's tomb, or our horses' feet injure their fields, we could not make out. Perhaps they were venting on our innocent heads some of the wrongs inflicted on them by our late companions, the Bashi-Bazouks.

We paused once more before entering the valley of Sychar, by the sacred ruined well. Except that sacred relic itself, all was unchanged. Down that narrow valley the woman came with her pitcher, whilst Jesus was resting on this well. The Saviour and the sinner met alone, and to her at first he was nothing more than a stranger and an alien from her race. Then followed that rapidly varying dialogue with its vivid imagery, taken, as so constantly in our Lord's conversations or sermons, from the things in sight at the time; the imagery so suddenly abandoned to flash the unexpected light on her conscience. Then the answer of the woman, betraying how, in hearts where no human eye would suspect a serious thought, deep religious perplexities may be dimly stirring, and how theological uncertainty and moral laxity accompany each other. Probably not a person in Sychar suspected that Samaritan woman of having a conscience, still less of weighing the merits of various religions, and expecting a Christ who would solve all difficulties. Was there, she seems to have thought, indeed, after all, a true faith to be found? The Jews believed one thing and her people another, and there might, perhaps, be much to be said on both sides; the balance of probabilities was pretty even, but might there, indeed, be One who would tell her absolutely which was right? There certainly was one before her, no empty disputant on her own level, speaking without authority, but "a prophet," who knew all her life, yet did not scorn to speak to her. To Him the secret perplexities of the doubting, sin-burdened heart came out.

Words, altogether new to her, came in reply. The controversy was carried to a higher level than her thoughts had reached. It was to be no more Jew or Samaritan; but God and adoring men and women. No more Gerizim, or Sion; but the Father and the human spirit.

One more secret lay in her heart. Through all that life of sin and doubt a dim desire and longing had lived on. The Christ was coming, the expectation of Jew and Samaritan alike. One who could answer all the heart's questionings was coming. One who could read all the heart's secrets was before her.

In words, at least, she made no inference, but all the secret aspirations of her soul were poured forth.

And she found the answer to which, perhaps, her heart had already almost sprung, "I that speak unto thee am He." Then, also down this valley, unless they had bought bread in that village on the hillside nearer, came back the disciples.

The woman had placed her pitcher by the well. It was not in her hands. She had not drawn any water for herself or for Jesus. But she had understood Him, as so few did. Water-pot, water, all were forgotten. There were men in Sychar who wanted the Christ as she had; there were hearts there who looked for him. She had good news to take. And up that valley, to the city out of sight behind the folding of those hills, sped her eager steps.*

---

* The other interpretation that the Samaritan woman intended *to turn the conversation* because it was *becoming too personal*, is surely unworthy. Could the

The disciples loved their Master, they had followed him faithfully; they had gone to buy him food while he rested. But when we turn from the Samaritan women to them, it is like turning from earnest, intelligent eyes which read your every glance, to a dull, prosaic countenance — beaming, indeed, with the best intentions, but understanding neither glance nor illustration, but exactly the literal words you say and no more. Jesus said, "I have meat to eat that ye know not of;" and the disciples, who had walked with him from Jerusalem, and listened for months to his teaching, of which almost every sentence was an illustration, had no idea that he could mean anything by "meat" but something to eat!

---

heart which had suddenly felt itself seen through and through possibly resort to such a wretched subterfuge? Let us take it rather as a proof of the thirst and void existing in the hearts of the worst, and be encouraged to spread these glad tidings.

Women and the Pharisees often understood our Lord best. The Pharisees, because their understandings were sharpened by dislike and fear, and "they knew he spoke those parables against them"; and women, because their hearts were warm,—they felt what he meant, felt that sinners might bathe his feet with tears; that he must help a mother whose young daughter was possessed, whether Phœnician or Hebrew: that he would welcome the love which broke the alabaster vase, and poured out the precious ointment.

I wonder if the disciples understood the next parable which our Saviour spoke, or perplexed themselves as to what he could mean by there being "four months to harvest," and yet the fields, so obviously green with the young corn, being "white already to harvest"?

Probably the eye of the Master directed them to the explanation, as, turning from the broad valley behind them, green with the young corn, He said, "*Lift up your eyes,* and look on the fields white for harvest," and as he said so glanced up the valley of Sychar, and watched the Samaritans coming to him, —the golden first-fruits of the harvest of the Gentiles.

They came down that deep valley, probably guided by the woman, no doubt conversing in eager groups as they came, and questioning and re-questioning her, on account of whose saying they had come. And when they reached the well where the Saviour and the disciples were still lingering, they besought him that he would tarry with them.

It was a new incident in that life spent among bitter enemies, and disciples so slow in understanding and heart. The people of Sychar had seen no miracle, they had heard none of those unequalled discourses. They had only heard that One sat on the well, at the opening of their valley, a stranger who saw with prophetic insight into the inmost heart and the past life, a Jew who did not scorn to have dealings with Samaritans. They came all that way in the evening from their city, simply because they had some dim hope of finding the Messiah there.

And when they found Him they recognized him. We do not read that he wrought any wonders among them. We might think it was impossible for him to come to any place without being troubled with compassion by its sorrows as well as by its sins, and healing bodies as well as souls. But we are told nothing of the kind. And for eighteen hundred years since then, his heart being the same, and his arm not shortened, he has been content, whilst healing souls, to let bodily sickness fulfil its work of discipline. Perhaps he could trust these Samaritans enough to treat them in the same way. He abode there two days.

Up this valley, which we were entering, He walked with that listening company and the wondering disciples. Beside this stream they went to that white cluster of flat-roofed houses, nestling among the thick trees.

Here, in the bosom of the hills, amongst the figs, pomegranates, and mulberries festooned with vines, on the fresh grass under the shade of the grey olives, and among the delicious sound of many waters, our Lord abode and taught for two days, and the Samaritans understood him as, perhaps, neither Pharisee nor apostle had yet done, to be not only indeed the Christ, but "the Saviour of the world."

It was Saturday evening as we rode up that lovely valley. Our tents were pitched outside the town under the thick shade of trees, amongst a chorus of streams flowing on every side. And here we were to remain for nearly two days, from Saturday until Monday.

I may add some lines which were written that Sunday at Nablous, to give some consolation for our great disappointment about the ruin of the well.

ON JACOB'S WELL RUINED BY THE ARABS.

They have stopped the ancient well,
Which the patriarchs dug of old;
Where they watered the patient flocks at noon,
From the depths so pure and cold.

Where the Saviour asked to drink,
  And found at noon repose;
But the Living Spring he opened there
  No human hands can close.

They have scattered the ancient stones
  Where at noon he sat to rest;
None ever shall rest by the well again
  And think how his accents blessed!

But the Rest for the burdened heart,
  The Shade in the wearied land,
The riven Rock with its living streams
  For ever unmoved shall stand.

Earth has no Temple now,
  No beautiful House of God;
Or Earth is all one Temple-floor
  Which those sacred feet have trod.

But in Heaven there is a Throne,
  A Home and a House of prayer:
Thyself the Temple, Thyself the Sun;
  Our pilgrimage endeth there!

Nablous, Sunday, June 22, 1856.

XI.

Sychar, Samaria,

AND THE PLAIN OF JEZREEL.

OUR tents were pitched close to Nablous, in a quiet place under the shade of trees, amidst the sound of many streams, fountains, and brooks that sprang out of valleys and hills.

Our slumbers were often broken that night by the dreary cries of the jackals, shrieking as they hunted over the hills, like children in pain.

The delight of remembering when we awoke the next morning that it was Sunday, and that we had nothing to do but to keep quiet, and feel ourselves in the city of the woman of Samaria, was great.

The clergyman in our party read the

English service. Never did the lessons and the old comprehensive prayers seem more touching and appropriate than on those Sunday halts on our way through Palestine.

A few peasants and towns'-people collected near us, and seated themselves on the ground at some little distance, during the service. We knew the feeling of the mob of Nablous was very excited just then against the Christians, but as we stood or knelt, and listened or responded, they offered us no interruption in any way, but quietly and contemplatively watched our proceedings.

In the afternoon we started for a walk, intending to reach the summit of Mount Gerizim, but our dragoman involved us in an unintentional call on the Keimakan, or governor of the town, which occupied us otherwise.

He led us first through the town of Nablous into the Samaritan quarter, where we saw the Samaritan synagogue. An ancient worn copy of the Pentateuch was taken out of its recess in the wall and shown us, but probably it was not the precious copy which the Samaritans of Nablous so jealously guard. This ancient Samaritan colony, however, is a commentary on New and Old Testament history, more interesting to unlearned eyes than any manuscript.

From this we were guided to the Keimakan's house, from the flat roof of which we were to have a good view of the valley. There, unfortunately for our walk to the top of Gerizim, the Keimakan's nephew met us, and invited me to pay a visit to the hareem. It would have been a discourtesy to decline, and, accordingly, I had to leave our party and descend a flight of steps from the roof to the women's apartments.

These steps led to an open court with a reservoir of pure water in the centre. Three ladies were sitting and standing in the court when the Keimakan's nephew took me there. One, who seemed to be the principal, invited me to sit down on some cushions which lay in the corner of a room opening into this court. Then they brought a Persian rug and spread it for me, and offered me a glass of sherbet. My large brown hat, with its folds of muslin coiled into a turban round it, amused them apparently as much as it would have our friends in England. They took it off, and stroked my hair, as one would a cat one wished to make friends with, and felt my dress. I showed them my eye glass, which entertained them greatly. Then I took a little child on my knee, which made a means of communication. So, with my few Arabic words we became very friendly. They offered me a chibouque, but I could not pretend to undertake an unmitigated long pipe; and not to offend them by declining their hospitality, I said, "Nargilleh." They then brought me a pipe twined like a snake round a glass jar full of rose-water, in which the bowl is placed, and I managed to create a few bubbles.

While this was preparing, another lady appeared who seemed the chief, as immediately all the others retired into the background and left me to my new hostess. She was quite caressing and affectionate, showed me into several bedrooms, unfastened the lattices which opened into the garden for me to look out, although she would not approach them herself, and finally placed me beside her on a divan in a room more furnished than any of the others, and had a nargilleh and a cup of coffee brought for me.

The rooms were very scantily furnished. Chairs and tables, of course, you could not expect; but there were no luxuries—no signs of women's work or taste, no flowers, sewing materials, or books, or traces of any kind of occupation or amusement—only four dreary white-washed walls, with a few cushions, and a recess in the wall closed with carved doors, for a wardrobe. The cushions were covered with chintz. Only in the room where I had coffee was a small Turkish table of ebony, inlaid with mother-of-pearl. The dress of the ladies was not as rich as I had expected, with the exception of rows of gold coins and pearls strung and festooned round their heads, as also around their children's. The loose veil and mantle which forms the out-door costume of the women, and enfolds them into a shapeless bundle of clothes, were, of course laid aside. The whole visit made me very sad. The position of those women, with their handsome expressive faces, and kindly lively caressing ways, weighed most painfully on my heart. And they were fellow-townswomen of the woman of Samaria! It was difficult to get away from them. At length, however, I made them to understand that I must not keep my party waiting, and succeeded in rejoining them on the roof of the house. There the Keimakan joined us, and was most polite. He was a grand-looking old man with a long white beard. His arrival involved a second edition of sherbet, pipes, and coffee, so that our walk up Gerizim was much abridged.

We climbed some way up, however, after taking leave of the hospitable governor, and were attended by a kawass, whom he insisted on our having, as a guide and escort. It was a pleasant path beside streams, occasionally crossing them, and always accompanied by their refreshing music, and among the luxuriant gardens and orchards which they water. The opposite hill, Ebal, looked comparatively bare and stony, only sprinkled with a little vegetation of a dull green. They told us the springs all rose on Gerizim,—the hill of blessing. If so it is a remarkably vivid type, the hill of cursing, barren, brown, and voiceless, — whilst the hill of blessing is clothed with evergreen herbage, luxuriant trees, and vines nourished by the living waters in its heart.

The remainder of the day we rested in or near our tents, and had time to think what those two days must have been in which our Lord once actually spent in this very place, listened to, welcomed, understood.

From this valley had gone up, eighteen hundred years ago, the first recognition of the Son of God, as not only the Jewish Messiah, the Christ, but the Desire of all nations, the Saviour of the world. One could fancy that the powers of life in nature had been unfettered here ever since, in virtue of that acknowledgment; and that the valley of Sychar was ever after to be a fragment and foretaste of paradise,—a place of streams and rest, full of all manner of trees pleasant to the eyes, and good for food, a little spot of earth visibly subject to the life giving sceptre of the "second Man," the Lord from heaven. No place to be compared with this in fertility and beauty exists, they say, in Palestine. We had, certainly, seen none.

It was pleasant, too, to think that this town and valley may also have been the one alluded to in the eighth of Acts,—the words translated in John iv., "a city of Samaria," and in Acts viii., "the city of Samaria," being the same. If so, this place was the first scene of a Samaritan Church, admitted by Peter and John, on the same level as the Church at Jerusalem. In this city there was then "great joy." And here again, no doubt (Acts xv.), as in the other Churches of Samaria, the tidings of the conversion of the

Gentiles in Asia Minor "caused great joy to the brethren," rejoicing that the Saviour of the world had at length been welcomed by the heathen world as once and for the first time in their own Samaritan city.

Thus the valley was full of happy and living associations, varied and refreshing as the sound of its own many waters.

On Monday morning some of our party walked again through the town, and saw a potter sitting at his wheel moulding the red clay into the simple, but picturesque bowls and pitchers used by the peasantry.

I longed to be able to speak to a few poor peasant women and children who came and sat by me under the shade of the mulberry-tree after our tents were struck. Fellow-townswomen of the woman in Samaria, surely the void and thirst in her heart existed also in theirs. If they could only have learned about the living water.

At three o'clock in the afternoon (Monday, June 30) we set off again, under the guard of two Bashi Bazouks sent by the Keimakan.

Reluctantly we ascended the hill out of that lovely valley, with its cool dewy atmosphere, its abundant streams, its fig-trees and mulberries, covered with vines, and its holy and happy memories.

After a pleasant ride of three hours over breezy hills we reached the place where our tents were pitched by a spring in a green valley just under the hill of Samaria.

Our route had now broken off, for an interval, from all definite incidents in the narratives of the Gospels, and in the history of the apostles. From Sychar to Nain, on the northern side of the Plain of Esdraelon, we are met by no name which recals any especial deed or word of our Lord. Yet the impress of his footsteps was with us everywhere. Again and again he had mounted these hills, and descended into these valleys, and crossed these hot and weary plains. There was one association which could never leave us, and on which it was almost a relief at times to fall back, after having our attention fixed keenly on some especial scene. The mere distances we traversed enabled us to realize in a way I had never done before, what the activity and fatigue of those three years of His ministry must have been.

He had traversed these paths on foot. It is evident that his journeys were not made in silence. The apostles were with him, and as they walked he taught them. Parable and proverb, and immortal sayings, and words of tender warning and sympathy, were always falling from his lips, as they went through vineyard, corn-field, or solitary path among the flickering shadows of the copse wood, or under the olive groves. And therefore, perhaps, it was only Jesus who was weary when they reached the well at Sychar.

It would be interesting to trace how many of our Lord's parables or instructions were given as they went in the way. "*As they went in the way* a certain man said unto him, Lord, I will follow thee whithersoever thou goest. And Jesus said unto him, Foxes have holes," the jackals which hunt about these hills by night have holes to hide themselves in by day, "and the birds of the air have nests, but the Son of man hath not where to lay his head."

Again, "Jesus going up to Jerusalem, took the disciples *apart in the way*, and said unto them, Behold, we go up to Jerusalem, and the Son of man shall be betrayed unto the chief priests and scribes; and they shall condemn him to death.'"

Again, "As *he went* through the cornfields on the Sabbath-day," the Pharisees found fault with the disciples for plucking the ears of corn; and he said unto them, "The Sabbath was made for man, and not man for the Sabbath."

Instances might be multiplied of this wayside teaching. Indeed, the number of the lessons of eternal truth called out by casual words or acts, or by the scenes he was passing through at the time, would probably far exceed our Saviour's more deliberate and formal instructions. It is this which gives the variety and vividness to his teachings. They were conversations, not "discourses." They were not put together as human words and works are; they *grew* as divine works do, and they live.

Of two incidents in the gospel we do, however, know that they happened among these Samaritan hills.

To one village in the country through which we were journeying, the Saviour of the world sent forward messengers to secure him a night's lodging. The name of the village is not given, any more than the name of the woman "who was a sinner." Sectarian bigotry prevailed over the common hospitality of the East. "They would not receive" One who was going up to the rival altar at Jerusalem. They did not know what that passover was to prove, nor who was to be its paschal lamb.

The fervent natures of the sons of thunder flashed into revengeful indignation. There must have been more fire in the eye of the beloved disciple, even in his chastened old age, than the mediæval painters have given him in youth. But the Lord turned and rebuked, not the inhospitable villagers, but the disciple whom he loved. He said to the brothers, "Ye know not what manner of spirit ye are of. For the Son of man is not come to destroy men's lives, but to save them." And quietly, uncomplainingly, without another word of comment, He for whom and by whom all things were created "passed on to another village."

This is the only incident recorded in the New Testament to the dishonor of the despised Samaritans. Perhaps the simple and touching story which we usually call the parable of the good Samaritan was actually a true narrative of a deed of kindness, marked by Him who observed the widow put her mite into the treasury, and saw Nathanael under the fig-tree. But however that may be, its scene was not in this immediate neighborhood.

The second incident of gospel narrative which may probably have occurred in Samaria, "as our Lord passed through Samaria and Galilee, on his way to Jerusalem," is the healing of the ten lepers. If this was so, somewhere on the rocky paths among those Samaritan hills our Lord's heart was gladdened by the sight of one grateful human being; and he, like the grateful woman of Sychar, was a Samaritan. One would like to identify, as much as any spot in Palestine, the place where the healed Samaritan leper, no more constrained, as an unclean person, to keep "afar off," fell down at the feet of Jesus, giving him thanks.

The more definite associations of the district around Samaria, interesting as they are, are scarcely sacred at all; and yet the situation of the city of Samaria is beautiful, and its ruins are more extensive than those of any other place in Palestine.

When we reached the stream at the foot of the hill of Samaria, beside which our tents were pitched, it was nearly sunset.

Flocks of sheep and goats were collected around the abundant, clear spring, to be watered from its large, rocky basin; and the women of the village of Samaria (Sebastiyeh) were filling their large earthen pitchers, to carry them up the winding road to their homes. As we rode up the hills, to see the ruins before the light was gone, we passed other women toiling under the weight of their heavy water-jars.

Samaria, like Nablous, and unlike most of the remaining cities in Palestine, retains the Greek name Herod gave it (Sebaste, Sebastiyeh), instead of its earlier Hebrew appellation. Its situation is indeed royal and beautiful, on the levelled summit of a rounded, isolated hill, separated by broad, fertile valleys from the higher hills around, through the openings of which it commands a very extensive range of distance. Its aspect must have been most queenly when the temples and palaces of the kings of Israel, and afterwards of Herod, crowned the platform at its summit, rearing their white columns and gilded roofs on the height to which the whole terraced hill must have seemed a magnificent flight of steps, tier above tier of terraces green with vines, silvery with olives, or golden with corn, leading the eye to the royal city at the summit.

Sixty or seventy columns are standing on the top of the hill, winding round in a double colonnade from near the remains of a massive, ancient gate, flanked with ruined towers. These columns were, we thought, monoliths, and some of them granite.

On the site of the city is an Arab village and many cultivated fields. The peasants were not very civil; but perhaps they were afraid we might prove tax-gatherers, deservedly their greatest terror next to the Bedouins.

A mosque, formerly a church, rises among these cabins. It is called the church of John the Baptist; and this tradition (naturally connecting the memory of the murdered prophet and the murderous king) points out as the scene of John the Baptist's death. Into the wall of this church is built a Corinthian column, probably from Herod's temple.

In the crypt underneath the church, shown to us as the prison and the tomb of John the son of Zachariah, is an ancient stone door, like some of those in the tombs of the kings at Jerusalem.

Before descending the hill we lingered to look at the magnificent panoramic view of mountains, rich plains, and wooded valleys, embracing a range east and west from the Mediterranean to the hills beyond Jordan which were burning that evening with all the glory of sunset. This was the view which was seen from the flat roofs of the palaces of Ahab and Herod. Some of our party saw jackals and a wolf within a hundred yards of them, on the site of Herod's city.

Such was the beauty of the place, and such its desolation. But what were its memories? They are not only disconnected with what is noblest in profane history, but almost entirely of the things that perish. Samaria was the metropolis, not of a nation dimly feeling its way to the light, but of one deliberately turning its back on a light not dimly revealed, and therefore the best human as well as all divine elements are absent from its records. Not only has it no David or Daniel or Hannah, but no Leonidas or Socrates.

No deed of true heroism or generous humanity consecrates its site any more than any life of true godliness. Its two conspicuous names are Ahab and Herod, the murderer of the blameless Naboth and the murderer of John the Baptist, the slaves of Jezebel and of Herodias. Its two most remarkable buildings were Ahab's temple of Baal, which Jehu destroyed, and Herod's temple to Augustus, whose columns are probably those among which we rode.

The connection of Elijah and Elisha with Samaria is scarcely an exception. They came to it, not as residents, but as prophetic visitants from the wilderness or the schools of the prophets, and usually with messages of doom. One single deliverance, indeed, characterizes Samaria—the panic which seized the besieging army of Benhadad, and laid open the richly furnished and provisioned tents of the Syrians to the four famishing lepers. A massive ancient gateway was, as has been said, the only ruin of importance which we remarked besides the colonnade, and we naturally fixed on it as the scene of that adventure, one of the most romantic (if the expression may be used) in the sacred narrative. We could imagine the hungry and so lately hopeless citizens passing through that rocky portal, at first in small groups, with slow and watchful movements, looking around on every side in fear of an ambush, and then, as party after party reached the camp, and not an enemy appeared, the sudden rise of confidence and the rush of the famished multitude through the narrow gateway, trampling down in their eager haste the sceptical official who tried to keep order among them. A feast ready spread for the famished, free range over their deserted hills for those who had been so long cooped up in hopeless inaction; yesterday a mother who had murdered her own child for hunger, and came to complain about it to the king, not as of a crime, but as of a bargain unfulfilled, all womanly feeling and all moral sense absorbed in the mad craving of hunger—and to-day, rescue, freedom, and plenty of every kind! History presents us with few more sudden and joyous contrasts, and yet we hear of no thank-offering, no song of praise. The godless spirit which displayed itself in scepticism in the nobleman, when Elisha prophescied deliverance, was manifested after the deliverance in the selfish, reckless haste of the people who trod him to death. Hopelessness in danger, selfish thankfulness in deliverance, the whole incident is a striking illustration how the alienation of men from God involves their alienation from one another.

The memories of Samaria are memories of crime, and idolatry, and of a splendor, all of "the earth, earthy," illumined by no true light of Divine truth or of human love. We descended the beautiful terraced hill without regret, and were very glad to find shelter in our little encampment in the valley, where a clear, abundant stream gurgled through the brushwood close to our tent-doors, tinkling over its pebbles, and eddying round its little shingly beaches, and giving us an unlimited supply of good water for all domestic purposes.

Through the night at times we heard the jackals wailing and screaming from the neighboring hills, and early in the morning the goats from a village near came to drink at the rocky basin which had just formed the bath for some of our party.

On the next morning (Tuesday, June 24th) we started at four o'clock. It was a beautiful ride. In many places the hills were cultivated; in almost all they might be clothed with luxuriant vegetation. We skirted the valley of Sebastiyeh, and as we climbed the opposite hills, and were winding through a pass leading into the Plain of Jezreel, we caught a last and most impressive view of the royal hill of Samaria. How often the city must have burst from this point on the sight of the Kings of Israel as they were returning from Jezreel!

For beauty few sites can equal it, and we could not help lingering to gaze and imagine how the royal city must have looked through this ravine, on its symmetrical isolated hill, with its crown of temples and palaces, and its queenly robe of terraced vineyards, cornfields, and olive gardens, sweeping majestically into the valley. But its temples were to Baal or to Cæsar, and its palaces were scenes of riot and crime. There was nothing to regret.

Soon afterwards we descended on the Plain of Jezreel, the great battle-field of Palestine, the inheritance of Asher. It was beautiful then, although the corn had been reaped. But in spring, after the rainy season, it must be delightful when the fields of young corn, their delicate green *shot* here and there with the tints of countless wild flowers, especially of the scarlet anemones, undulates like a sea as far as the eye can reach on each side, running up among the hills and headlands in long creeks and spreading bays of living verdure.

Unfortunately for the inhabitants, this rich plain has many an outlet through the Jordan valley into the Desert, and the Bedouins, with their camels and black tents, make inroads on it now as easily as their ancestors, the Midianites of old. There are few places on this side of the Jordan so perilous to travellers as Esdraelon. About mid-day we reached Jenin (Engannim, the well of gardens), a place of springs and gardens still. Our thirsty horses soon scented the water, and quickened their steps to reach the extensive troughs, where large flocks of pretty, long-eared goats and sheep, with herds of cattle such as we had not seen for a long time, were being watered. From these abundant and well-kept wells, we were directed to a garden, where they spread mats for us, under the shade of a magnificent mulberry-tree, the fruit of which dropped around us. We were regaled on mulberries, figs, cucumbers, and tomatos. Soon after this an

American and a Dutchman came, with mules and horses, and pitched their tent under the same mulberry. Then we discovered that Jezreel, where we had intended spending the night, was not a safe place of encampment, on account of the Bedouins, and as no other halting-place was within reach, provided with springs, and uninfested with these desert marauders, we had to find another garden, and encamp for the day and night at Jenin.

Although we regretted at the time the "annexation" of our mulberry by the strangers, we afterwards much preferred our second resting-place, because it was under the shade of a garden at the edge of the plain, and gave us a fine uninterrupted view over the whole broad level, with its occasional islands of hill, and its reaches of fertile land stretching past headland after headland of its mountain coasts.

Hither, from the height of Tabor, unseen on the north, Deborah and Barak's patriotic band had swept down on the hosts of Sisera, encamped with chariots and horsemen on the western reaches of Esdraelon, and routed them in the battle of Megiddo.

Hither, from their deserts in the East, the Midianites and the Amalekites, and the children of the East, had come up and pitched in this valley or plain of Jezreel, with their cattle and their tents. This broad level, where now we only saw the waving of thin vegetation springing up after the harvest, was alive with their camels and their cattle, and the movements of their horsemen scouring the plains for plunder, "like the sand by the sea-side for multitude." The whole land was astir with them, as the fields at evening with the hum of countless cicadas or "grasshoppers." And through those passes on the east their chieftains and all the scattered host fled after Gideon's victory.

On the "high places" of Gilboa, on the north-east, Saul and Jonathan fell by the hands of the Philistines, and were lamented by David in the pathetic dirge we know so well.

From the range of Carmel on the west, Ahab drove into Jezreel, the girded prophet Elijah running with supernatural swiftness before him. And before they reached the city, the little cloud rising from the Mediterranean not larger than a man's hand, had covered the whole sky with blackness, and was pouring down its torrents of blessing on these mountains and this plain. What a miraculous change the few days after that rain must have made in the scenery around us! Long-buried and forgotten seeds of life, flowers, and corn, and grasses, springing up on hill-side, valley, and level, till all the land was one tide of exuberant life.

We were in the region of chariots. Here the Syrian hosts of Benhadad, with chariots and cavalry, had filled the country, and across this level sweep they had fled before the Israelites, who had been pitched before them, " like two little flocks of kids," because the blaspheming of the Syrians might not pass unanswered, that the God of Israel was a local deity, such as they believed their own to be, "a god of hills, but not of the plains." Across this plain, not long afterwards, Jehu was seen driving his chariot furiously from the border land of Gilead, to execute vengeance on the doomed house of Ahab.

And from that time to this, the corn fields of Esdraelon have been trampled down by Bedouin tribes and invading armies, "children of the East," and children of the West. The villages and towns which lie (like the villages on the coasts of Genoa) on the sides of the headlands which bound the plain, or crown the little hills which rise here and there like islands from it, have looked down from age to age on scene after scene of war and slaughter. The records of its battles range from the book of Judges to the Revelation; from the rout of the armies of Sisera at Megiddo, the western branch of this plain, to the battle of the great day of God Almighty, when the kings of the earth and the whole world are gathered together into a place "called in the Hebrew tongue Armageddon." Whatever may be the meaning of that last announcement in the Apocalyptic vision, this final allusion cannot but give a deep and mysterious interest to the great battle-field, beneath whose sod such countless numbers of warriors already lie, and which furnishes the title for the last great conflict, which, we are promised, shall be a victory for the Prince of peace.

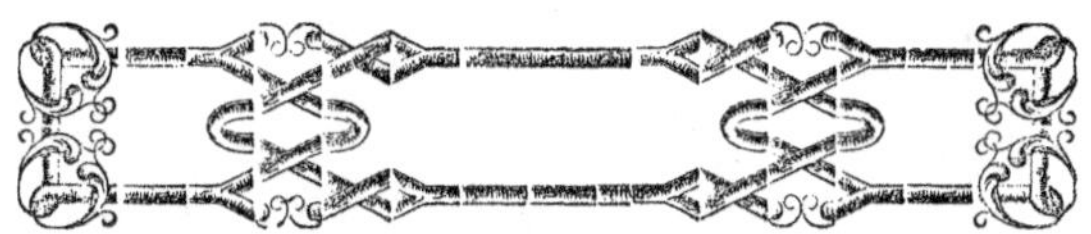

XII.

Shunem, Nain and Nazareth.

EARLY in the morning of Wednesday, the 24th June, our little encampment in the garden of the Fountain Gardens (Engannim) was broken up again, the tents were struck, our hasty breakfast of eggs and coffee was finished, and we set off once more across the plain of Jezreel without prospect of a shelter from the scorching sun, except such as we might find under tree or rock, until evening, when we hoped to rest in the Latin Convent of Nazareth.

Our first point was Zerin, the ancient Jezreel, now a collection of poor Arab huts. It is situated, like other villages on the plain of Esdraelon, on a slight elevation which commands a fine view across the level, from the fertile and wooded range of Carmel on the west, to the valley of the Jordan on the east, the isolated heights of Tabor rising in the distance on the north. The dogs howl and prowl around it as they do around all Arab villages, and as they did in the days of Jezebel and Ahab, and of the murdered Naboth.

It is remarkable how even the intermittent and feeble adherence of Judah to God gave a stability to its metropolis and its government which the transient and arbitrary dynasties of the ten separated tribes never knew.

Jerusalem was supreme and unrivalled among all the cities of Judah, as the house of David among all the families of Judah; but in the history of Israel how often the metropolis is changed; oftener even than the dynasty.

Bethel might attract the tribes sometimes when they desired to wrench some selfish advantage by mercenary sacrifices from indifferent or reluctant Powers, but it was no centre of national unity. Shechem and Tirzah and Samaria and Jezreel were royal residences, rather than national cities. No heroic or patriotic songs are inspired by these names, still less any sacred psalms. They are mere Versailles, with pleasure-grounds and "Naboth's vineyards," but with no Acropolis and no Temple—idling places of a court, not rallying points of a race. What Jewish heart in exile ever wailed, "If I forget thee, O Samaria"? With the Temple and the city of God the history of the ten tribes seems to lose all its patriotic interest, and to become little more than the record of a Persian satrapy, or a series of Egyptian dynasties; little more, and therefore far less, inasmuch as all gifts of God rejected, degrade by the measure to which they might have raised.

The events of national interest connected with this portion of Palestine seem confined to the period before the parting of the stream into the two channels; the descent of Barak's patriotic band from Tabor, the victory of Gideon, the flight and capture of the Midianitish chieftains, the defeat and death of Saul and Jonathan on the high places of Gilboa, bewailed in David's generous dirge. From the period of the disunion the interest of the national history, religious festivals, reformations, patriotic conflicts, desperate clinging to the ancestral city even in its desecration, all are concentrated in Judah. Whatever of interest lingers about the ten tribes gathers around individual narrative, biographies of persecuted prophets, stories of humble home life. The sacred names of Israelitish history are not Samaria and Jezreel, but Carmel, Sarepta and Shunem. The rents in the national Jewish life, however, let the light stream through on the great Gentile world beyond, and it is significant that the only narratives quoted by our Lord in connection with the history of Israel are those of the widow of Sarepta and the Syrian leper.

But perhaps the most touching and familiar story connected with the later history of Israel is that of the "great woman" of

Shunem, which place was our next halting point after Jezreel. The characters are so attractive, the incidents so touching, the details so minute, and the end of the story so happy, that it rises like a strain of joyous singing, or like an illuminated fragment of gospel narrative from the dreary chronicles of the houses of Jeroboam, Ahab, and Jehu.

The village of Solem (Shunem) is situated on the side of a hill, forming part of the range of Little Hermon and Gilboa. Belonging to it were some luxuriant gardens of lemons and oranges, such as we had not seen since leaving Jaffa and the maritime plain. They were enclosed with fences of prickly pear.

After passing these orange gardens, we came to an abundant spring, welling up cold and pure from a cavern in the hill-side. A number of the villagers gathered around us with a friendly curiosity, and one kindly looking woman offered me a draught of water from her pitcher, and made no request for backsheesh in return. We thought the spirit of the hospitable Shunammite must linger around the place.

Somewhere near this fountain and these orange gardens, the "little chamber" had actually arisen on the wall of the house of that open hearted Jewish gentlewoman, so womanly in the thoughtful care which set the bed, and the table, and the candlestick; so princely, in the refusal of all return. She needed no favor from court or camp. She could receive no reward for care so freely bestowed. She dwelt among her own people.

Then the child's voice coming to gladden the household; the new mother's love with all its possibilities of sorrow; the boy returning from his manly occupations in the sultry harvest field, and drooping in the summer noon, and dying on his mother's knee; the little chamber entered with the mournful burden of that precious corpse laid on .the bed, prepared with such kindly care of old for the man of God; the chamber door shut on the silence of death; the grief which found no utterance except in action until the prophet was reached; the rapid ride across the long reaches of the plain from Gilboa to Carmel, with the complaint which could be trusted to no messenger or mediator, but must burst straight from the mother's lips to the heart of the man of God himself; the quick sympathy of the prophet, who saw through the "It is well," which was all she vouchsafed to Gehazi, how her soul was "bitter" within her; the officious formality of the selfish Gehazi, deeming that the dignity of heavenly messengers must be fenced by courtly etiquette from too fervent petitions; the miserable unsympathizing coldness of the man who knew much of the forms of religion, and nothing of the heart of God. How, indeed, could the prophet's staff in his hand have awakened the dead child? The prophet did not use the staff. It was through no cold mechanical medium he drew the life from God, which he communicated to the boy. He shut the door upon them twain; he prayed unto the

Lord, and eye to eye, mouth to mouth, warm living hands on the cold dead hands, he stretched himself, until the dead waxed warm with the life ot the living, and the child opened his eyes, and the mother was sent for, and with a joy apparently as unutterable in its intensity as her sorrow had been, "fell at the prophet's feet, and took up er son and went out."

Love, with its lowly common necessities and sorrows, had come to break up the princely calm of the Shunammite lady's life, and henceforth she was to be tossed about on the sea of our common human hopes and fears, and could no more say, "I have need of nothing."

When the seven years' famine came, she fled at Elisha's warning into the land of the Philistines, and when she returned she sought his intercession with the king, and obtained the restitution of her lost inheritance, the inheritance of her son, among these hills and plains, and among these gardens of Shunem. To her as to us, God's most precious earthly gifts are not those which land the heart in a haven of rest, or smooth it into an even surface of ease, or fill it with a little quieting draught of comfort; but those which launch the heart on the seas, where it is tossed and strained, and finds goodly pearls,—those which upturn its depths, and water them, and make them fruitful. The man of God had not deceived her, or given her a stone for bread. Nor will God do so to us.

From Shunem we crossed the shoulder of Little Hermon to the poor little village of Nain, where we made our mid day halt in the court-yard of one of its hovels, under the shadow of its one olive tree. The rest was very welcome on the breezy hill-side.

The owner of the poor cabin was friendly, and brought us coffee in a tiny cup, thick, according to Turkish custom, as chocolate, but very refreshing. Two or three bright-eyed boys gathered around us. I volunteered to mend one of their very simple garments; and they were in ecstasies when they discovered the secret of our coasting glass' and found the sheep on a distant hill brought quite close, so that altogether we parted very good friends.

A few poor cabins, on the steep hill-side, one olive among them, a little below, a well with one green tree near it, and a few ruins, or scattered stones,—and this is Nain.

The transition from Shunem to Nain seems easy and natural. You could scarcely find two points at which Old and New Testament history more easily coalesce than in the two narratives which hallow these two villages, situated so near each other on the opposite sides of the same hill. The names of both are preserved unmistakeably in the language of the peasants, unperplexed by any monastic traditions.

Again, it is a story of life and death and life restored, and of an only son.

This poor little village was a "city" then—a town with walls and gates, and multitudes of inhabitants, many of whom thronged out of the gate with the funeral procession which wound down the steep side of the hill to the burial-ground outside the walls. For nearly two millenniums now every one of the multitude who followed that one dead fellow-townsman have passed away to the bourne from which he only ever returned. Probably they all lie buried, that busy throng, in the cave-tombs beneath this hill to which they were bearing him. And every vestige of their life has vanished except the memory of that one funeral, which has made their dwelling-place a household word in Christian homes all over the world. The procession was issuing from the gate down this hill-side —not silently, and with slow, measured step, as on such an occasion among us, but lamenting loud and passionately, with hurried steps and rent garments, weeping, and pouring forth that terrible, piercing wail as they went —the open bier borne on the heads of the bearers—amongst them one broken hearted, desolate woman, who probably did not wail, but only wept—when they met the company around Jesus entering the city; a larger group than usual, for the day before, the centurion's servant had been healed at Capernaum, and "many of his disciples went with him, and much people."

Then came one of those revelations of the heart on whose love the universe depends, which ought to have silenced for ever all those negative definitions of a Being too sublime to feel, at which our hearts shiver and fold up into themselves.

"When the Lord saw her, he had compassion on her." It was no exceptional compassion, no mere capacity of sympathy, put on with his human nature; it was the divine pity which, though now first beamed or wept through human eyes, is the same from everlasting to everlasting in the heart of the eternal Father and the eternal Son of his love—the same now, not measuring our sorrows by his infinity, but by our suffering. In a few minutes the cause of the widow's tears would be removed; but his words of sympathy, "Weep not," anticipated the work of mercy. His touch arrested the bier; his voice reached the dead. It was not the first time the dead had been won back to life among those hills. Yet how different the character of the miracle!

In the little silent chamber, with the closed door, in the house at Shunem, on the opposite side of the hill, Elisha had prayed and contended in God's strength with death. His prayer was heard, and through the living prophet life flowed from God into the dead child. The prophet called on God, because God knew his voice. He did not call on the dead. His voice would not have reached that invisible world. But at Nain how different! How tranquil and majestic the bearing of the Son of God! No effort, no recorded prayer, no tonch; but simply the imperial, divine, "I say unto thee, arise," from the voice which penetrated into the world of spirits, and recalled the disembodied soul from Hades, as easily, as gently as a mother's voice awakes a sleeping child. At Shunem it was the living in contract with the dead. At Nain it was the life-giving, the Life himself, laying his irresistible command on death itself, the last enemy.

And great fear came on all. They must have felt, for the hour at least, that the Person was more wonderful than the miracle.

"Jesus delivered him to his mother." The heart that had been moved with compassion by her tears cared for her joy. Let us treasure up those traces of his love, and let us not say only when we think of them, "How human our Saviour was!" This love, this tender pity, this caring for our transitory joys and sorrows, are divine; divine far more than human; and only human because they were first divine.

At Nain, after our rest, we remounted, and after passing a well where they were watering a flock of graceful, long-eared goats, crossed another reach of the plain of Esdraelon. Tabor rose on our right, and beyond the low ridge which connected Tabor with the surrounding hills, towered the distant, snow-streaked Hermon. The plain was partially tilled, and was covered in many places with a waving plant, with a prickly, starry flower, and bluish leaves, which, in the distance, had the effect of long rippling pools of water.

Every detail of the scenery gathered a deeper interest as we advanced, for we were fast approaching the home of our Lord's early human years; the scenery through which he had not merely passed on his rapid, toilsome journeys, but amongst which he had lived for nearly thirty tranquil secluded years. That night we were to sleep at Nazareth.

Slowly, after leaving the plain, we rode up, winding through the valley under what is traditionally called "The Mount of Precipitation," to the fountain known as the Fountain of the Virgin. The fountain now flows beneath a stone arch, through a marble spout, into a large stone trough like a sarcophagus, and thence trickles away. It is an abundant spring of good water, and many of the women of Nazareth were gathered around it, talking, as they waited for their pitchers to fill, at the evening hour when we passed it. We enjoyed a draught from it, and had no doubt that, eighteen hundred years ago, one maiden of Nazareth, "blessed among women," used to take her quiet way down that winding road to this very spring. And, in after years, did not the feet of the "child Jesus" actually tread the same path?

Of all places in the world I had almost longed to see this most. It seemed as if the sight of the scenery of that home at Nazareth would help more than anything to fill up the silence of those long, unrecorded years. And now at length this little secluded hollow of the Galilean hills, which had cradled the childhood of our Saviour, opened on us; a little quiet valley, or basin, surrounded by hills on all sides, except at the narrow pass from the plain of Esdraelon, through which we entered it; a village shut out from the world; white houses, partly nestled in the bottom of the hollow, and partly, on one side, climbing the hills, which, in that place are steep and craggy, —the hill on which the city was built.

We rode through the streets to the Latin Convent—a large white building, with flat roof, and long airy corridors, where we lodged during the two nights we remained, willingly exchanging our tents for the hospitality of the monks, and their large, cool, clean rooms.

Before breakfast the next morning we all rode with Mr. Huber, the Protestant missionary, around the environs of Nazareth. As we left the village at that early hour, we saw, through an open door, two women grinding at a mill in the court-yard of a house. From the heights above we had a magnificent view, from Carmel on the west, stretching its green and wooded heights into the blue Mediterranean, over the high tableland above the sea of Galilee, to Tabor on the east, dotted thickly with trees and green to its level isolated summit, and Hermon, pale in the distance, with its silvery streaks of snow. It was a rough ride, over rocky fields, and through terraced olive gardens and vineyards, sadly ruined and wasted by the Bedouins and the Turkish soldiers. The views changed continually, and were very beautiful. The hills were much more varied in form than the round monotonous heights in the south of Palestine, near Jerusalem. We had not seen anywhere in the Holy Land such really mountain landscapes. The long waving wooded range of fruitful Carmel, with all the hills and valleys between it and Nazareth, dotted here and there with white villages, and sprinkled with clusters of trees, contrasted with the symmetrical isolated hill of Tabor, and that again with the long, pale, snow-streaked ridge of Hermon and the Lebanon. The valleys also were as varied as the hills, from the quiet oval hollow of Nazareth itself, with its corn-fields and olives, through the countless slopes, and dells, and little plains between us and the Mediterranean, to the long, ocean-like sweep of Esdraelon on the south, beautifully green (Mr. Huber told us) in spring with corn. In one olive-garden we dismounted to look at an olive-oil press, a cistern hollowed in the solid rock of the hill-side, and connected by a groove, or channel, with another deeper cistern cut out of the rock below, into which the oil flowed as it is trodden out of the olives. Any little details of domestic life had peculiar interest at Nazareth.

We returned to the convent by the steep side of the hill, up which climbed the houses of Nazareth, tier above tier. Many people believe this to have been the brow of the hill on which the city was built, from which the people sought to cast our Lord down. It seems more probable than that they should have taken him more than a mile up the hills to the traditional Mount of Precipitation. The hills of the valley in this point are, in some places, precipitous and craggy.

In the afternoon, some of our party took a second ride over the surrounding country to one of the two villages, supposed to be the Cana of the miracle. But we preferred relinquishing this expedition for the unspeakable delight of a quiet ramble on foot alone over the hills in the immediate neighborhood of Nazareth. We rambled and rested several hours on those breezy quiet hills, aromatic with the fragrant thyme, which the bees of the land of milk and honey love. On the top of the hills the air seemed like a sea-breeze, so fresh and reviving; probably, indeed, it was a breeze steeped in the freshness of the Mediterranean which we had seen from the higher ground that morning. The varied foldings of these hills form many quiet nooks, as lonely as if you were in the desert, —in the desert-place to which, in after years, He went a great while before day to pray. Just round the shoulder of the steep which Nazareth climbs, you lose sight of every trace of the village. Many lovely wild-flowers grow on the heights, sea-pinks, a little delicate blue blossom like the nemophila, brilliant scarlet poppies, the graceful wild convolvulus, and others not so familiar to us. But the burst of beauty among the wild-flowers follows close on the rainy season, and this was past when we were there.

We paused chiefly at two points on the hills to look, and sketch, and rest. One was a height just above the "brow of the hill on which the city was built," looking down an abrupt descent on the white roofs of the Latin Convent, some houses of considerable size, across the narrow valley to the opposite hills broken here and there into terraces, earth, and rocks, brown and warm in tint, with clusters of grey olives among them, and the isolated top of Tabor towering alone behind and above the range of hills which immediately bound the valley.

As we walked from this spot we saw a group of children clustered under an olive. It was a school, and we admired the taste of the master in the selection of their study, and wondered whether he knew how to give them lessons from the "lilies of the field" and "the fowls of the air." A little further up, the broad western landscape opened to us, hill beyond hill, village and corn-field, and olive groves, to Carmel, and the golden line of the Tyrian sands meeting the blue waves of the "great sea."

Our second resting-place was at the head of the hollow or basin of Nazareth, which, as before mentioned, has no outlet except at the lower end towards Esdraelon. Here we were near the ruined vineyards we had ridden over in the morning, and commanded the whole length of the valley. Just below us, was the flat roof of the Greek convent on the traditional site of "the House of the Virgin;" beyond it, on the left, a group of people thronging around a well. At our elevation we could hear no sound, but on visiting this well afterwards, we found its scanty and badly-managed water a scene of the most violent quarrelling among the women of the village for the right of the first turn. At that height, however, all this was inaudible, or only reached us in a broken hum. On the hill-side on the right, the flat-roofed houses rose half hidden amongst trees, and conspicuous among them the white minaret of a mosque gleamed like ivory amidst its black cypresses. Beyond the village stretched, in the perspective of the valley to its termination, a long range of golden corn-fields, broken at intervals by the olive groves which swept down across them from the hills. The valley ended in the cleft of the hills through which we had ascended from the plain, and beyond this stretched the broad sweep of Esdraelon, level as the sea. bounded in the far distance by the undulating line of the hills beyond Jordan, the land of Gilead. At that hour every thing was bathed in its loveliest light. Hill, and valley, and corn-field, and the distance glowed in the warm evening tints, and the long, broken shadows of the hills, were thrown at intervals across the valley of Nazareth.

We knew we must not trust the brief twilight, and hastened to return over the broken terraces of the ruined vineyards. That afternoon walk was one of the brightest memories of the HolyLand ; and yet how is it possible to transfer the impression of a delight which consisted chiefly in *being there*, in gathering the common wild flowers on those hills, in feeling their fragrance, in watching the common changes of sun and shade, and day and evening on those scenes, in walking on the rough rocks and broken clods of earth, and breathing the breezy air, and feeling with every sense that Nazareth, the home of the Son of God for thirty years, is no dream-land, but actually a place on this common everyday earth.

On our way back to the Latin Convent we came on another olive or wine-press, hewn out of the solid rock, with a pit ten feet deep to receive the oil or wine, and crossed several tanks and terraced vineyards, all now disused, and waste, and ruined.

We have no "Gospel of the Infancy" like that early apocryphal book which is said by the contrast of its absurd stories to form such a commentary on the divine origin of the genuine narrative. Our only "Gospel ot the Infancy" and childhood of our Lord is contained in two short sentences, "He grew in favor with God and and man," and "He was subject unto them." Brief but vivid traces of those many years of love and service. Two brief sentences;—and Nazareth. This is all we know. But in the silence of the Book, the Land speaks to us with peculiar power, through the scenery of the daily life of that sacred home whose history is concealed with so thick a veil. In the absence of the record of words and acts, it is something to fill those years with the pictures of the breezy hills, the deep secluded valley, the wide prospects across the land from Gilead to the sea,—the glimpses of Tabor and distant snowy Hermon, the mountain landscapes and the lonely nooks on the hill-sides, fragrant with thyme and bright with flowers, among which those years were spent.

What thoughts those wide views of hill, valley, Galilean villages, the distant Tyrian shore, the great battle-field of Esdraelon, and Hermon with garments "white as no fuller on earth can white them" awakened in the Redeemer's heart, and what prayers those silent hills have witnessed, the rest of the gospel narrative may tell us. Tiberias, the Mount of Transfiguration, Olivet, Gethsemane, Calvary, give us abundant comments on the silent pictures of Nazareth.

XIII.

Tabor and the Sea of Galilee.

EARLY in the morning, on Friday, the twenty-seventh of June, we left the Latin Convent at Nazareth to resume our tent life. We had quitted no place in the Holy Land with more longing to linger there. But if we had staid a year instead of a day, we must still have left with regret; and unless a visit can be prolonged into a residence, a few extra days, perhaps, scarcely add much to the force of recollection. The vividness of the first impression wears off, and there is not time to replace it by the familiarity of daily associations, so that what is lost in freshness, is scarcely compensated by what is gained in acquaintance with detail. At all events, we tried to console ourselves with considerations of this kind, as we wound our way over the hills which separate from the world the mountain cradle of the life which has transformed the face of the world, and renewed the depths of every Christian's life.

It was very early in the morning when we started. The sun had scarcely risen. The long shadows of the hills lay across the valleys ; the air was breezy and cool ; our horses, especially the little nimble white horse I rode, were fresh and eager after their day of comparative rest, and paced quickly over the downs, and valleys, and wooded hills.

For the hills on that morning ride from Nazareth to Tabor might really be called wooded, especially as we approached Tabor. Not that the hills were clothed with those rich masses of wood which, in the moist atmosphere of England, often make the distant hills look purple, and soft as the plumage of a dove; but our path lay under the frequent shadow of oaks of various kinds, and terebinth, and luxuriant thorn-trees. Many green and glossy shrubs grew as brushwood in the intervals, and the ground beneath them was often strewn with wild flowers which scented the morning air; thyme, pink convolvulus, a large blue thistle-like flower, and a deep blue prickly star. It was not a forest certainly, but it often recalled the scenery at the outskirts of an English park; trees and evergreen shrubs with shining leaves, standing apart, with full liberty for the development of each, and branches feathering to the ground; with flowers and green, flowering shrubs between and among them.

The oaks increased in size as we approached Tabor, and grew closer to each other, yet still you could not so much say the hill was clothed with wood as thickly sprinkled with trees, clustered in park-like groups, or scattered here and there, as on the edge of a felled coppice. The path up the hill was very steep and rocky, in many parts rather perilous, winding among the rocks and the roots of the trees. In some places we had to climb rough staircases of rock, as on the hill road from Jaffa to Jerusalem; while in others we rode along green glades and terraces, shaded with oak and terebinth, and sprinkled with syringa and other flowering shrubs. As we approached the summit, the bridle path widened into a carriage road, which had been hewn in the solid rock. There were grooves of chariot wheels deeply worn in this road, certainly not traversed by chariots for many centuries—probably not, at the latest, since Roman times. It led to a massive gateway; and on the summit of Tabor, to my great surprise, we found ourselves among the extensive ruins of ancient fortifications.

No place in the Holy Land more contradicted my previous image of it than did Tabor. From childhood, I suppose, most of us have pictured it a solitary mountain, on whose green pastures the flocks peacefully graze, whose brow rises quiet and lonely to the sky. Mountains in our northern climates give the idea of calm solitude, above the din and turmoil of the lower world. Even if not peaked with wild rocks or crowned with snow, the last idea one connects with a mountain-top is that of a city. Yet the summit of Tabor must evidently have been, not a mere fortress or military station, but a city. We had been accustomed to look on the low rounded hills of southern Palestine as pedestals for towns or villages, and we had admired the regal site of Samaria on its isolated hill; but Tabor is not a hill, but a mountain, eighteen hundred feet above the sea, and rising more than thirteen hundred feet above the land immediately surrounding it. The walls have been very massive, and the fortifications very strong, as an engineer officer in our party assured us. A deep fosse surrounds the wall on the least precipitous side of the mountain. Along the walls, at intervals, were the ruins of towers. One of these had pointed arches in the doors and windows, and had, probably, been built or repaired in crusading times. Others seemed far more ancient; and some of the gigantic stones in the walls appeared to be of Jewish or Phœnician workmanship. Underneath the walls and towers we explored a very large reservoir or water tank, lined with cement; several cisterns, smaller, but still of considerable size, shaped like bottles, with the long narrow neck upwards; and some magazines apparently intended for corn or various military stores. Broken pottery lay around in these subterranean reservoirs, and great evergreen oaks grew from the interstices of the massive stones, which their gigantic roots had here and there displaced, and threw their broad broken shadows over the deserted chambers. Altogether, with the trees, and verdure, and large-leaved plants which sprang out of the crevices of the broken masonry, it reminded us of a ruined castle on the Rhine, such as Rhemfels. But the ruins on Tabor are not those of a castle but of a city, and the date of the latest is probably about that of the earliest of those fastnesses of robber or crusader on the Rhine. In one part we came on the remains of a church, lately partially repaired by the Greeks as a place of pilgrimage, and, perhaps, previously repaired by the Crusaders from the earlier Greeks.

The peculiar feature of the ruins, however, is that they enclose a large space of green level ground, on which there is no trace of buildings of any kind. It must have been a strongly fortified town encircling a spacious park. This green and wooded platform is considerably lower than the edges of the hill, whose height is increased by the ruins of the fortifications. The summit of the mountain seemed to us to form something like a volcanic crater, whose edges were walled; although Tabor is not volcanic, but a limestone spur of the hills of Galilee.

We supposed it must have been a place of refuge, to which in times of war or danger, the inhabitants of the surrounding villages fled for protection, encamping in the park-like space within the city with their cattle. An impregnable place of refuge it must have been in the days of arrows and slings, commanded or even approached by no neighboring height, and containing such ample space for stores, and even—if needed—for the tillage of crops.

Our saddle bags were opened under the shade of the oaks, and we sat as long as we could venture to linger among the trees and ruins ; the thick foliage, the long grass and wild flowers stirring and rustling in the breeze around us, and the whole of northern and southern Palestine at our feet in successive landscapes, as we moved from point to point along the edge of the hill, and rested on the massive stones of the more ancient fortifications. In winding round the mountain on our way up, we had caught various glimpses of the plains below, of the villages of Endor and Nain, and over Esdraelon to Jordan and the Mediterranean. On the summit we kept chiefly to the side which commanded the north, and saw from the hills of Galilee across the high table-land above Tiberias, to the sea of Galilee, the gleam of whose waters just caught the eye in the distance, sunk in their deep basin below the plain. Beyond rose the long back of Hermon, from that point not rising in one grand distinctive summit, but stretching in a long undulating line, pale with distance, but quite clear, and streaked—not crested—with silvery lines of snow. Hermon from Tabor was not a sight we could easily leave; yet the unexplored country beyond us, the hills and lake of Galilee were, if possible, more interesting than these. We traced one or two streams across that hot brown plain by their border of verdure, and occasional clusters of olives, and we could see too plainly how considerable was the distance yet to be traversed that day, to admit of our lingering more than a few hours.

We descended the hill by a rocky road, over part of which we thought it safer to walk, leaving our gentle, sure-footed little horses to follow.

Barak and his brave ten thousand were on foot when they assembled on this mountain, and poured down its rocky side upon Jezreel, sweeping the cavalry and chariots of the Canaanites across the plain to Kishon and the sea. Cavalry would certainly have availed little on those broken wooded steeps. It was inspiriting to think how the war cries of the little Israelitish army must have resounded from these rocks as they rushed on, irresistible with the prophecies of Deborah and the arm of the Lord.

But there was one event commonly associated with Tabor, which would indeed pale the interest of all others if it occurred here. Can it be that on some secluded terrace of this wooded hill, the glory of the Son of God for the time broke through the veil, and the garments "white as no fuller on earth can white them," and the face "shining as the sun," once beamed forth here through the night on the three wonder-stricken apostles?

At first the existence of this ancient fortress or fortified town on the summit of Tabor seems so to contradict the natural impression of the narrative, as to preclude the possibility of this mountain having been — as tradition makes it—the scene of the Transfiguration. There are and were so many solitary and even desert hills in and near Galilee, that one cannot easily conceive the close neighborhood of such a stronghold as this to have been the spot chosen for a manifestation, so zealously veiled from the eyes, and at first guarded from the knowledge of all but the three. Yet Tabor is a mountain — not a mere ordinary hill — and on its rocky sides, doubtless, many a place absolutely secluded might always have been found, especially at night, when it is most probable the event happened. St. Peter's expression, "the holy Mount," implies nothing. The Presence consecrated the place. Many think Hermon the most probable scene, chiefly influenced, it would seem, by the far greater majesty of the scenery of Hermon, its sublime mountain solitudes, and the constant presence, on its lofty clefts, of the snow, to which the glistening transfigured garments are compared.

But when narratives so circumstantial and simple as those of the three Gospels avoid every detail which could lead to a positive identification of the place, is it not probable that this indefiniteness is deliberate and designed? All topographical details which could give vividness and reality to the incidents, are in the New Testament so carefully specified, and at the same time all curious indications which might lead to a superstitious identification of certain precise spots, are so systematically omitted, that there is no point more frequently pressed on one's attention in the Holy Land than this: that Christianity, whilst as a history of facts capable of standing the strictest tests of geography, as a revelation of truths and of a divine life, vouchsafes no assistance to the spirit of superstitious pilgrimage.

At Jerusalem, you can feel with certainty that your feet are treading the foot-path to Bethany, that you are wandering along the olive shaded valley where the garden of Gethsemane was, that you are standing on the very same sacred temple precincts where the blind and lame came to Jesus and were healed. But on what spot of that valley the forehead of our Lord was bowed in agony, or on what part of the hilly ground close to the walls of the city fell the precious drops of His redeeming blood no human being knows.

Again, at Nazareth you can roam about the breezy, thyme-scented hills, and be absolutely sure you are gazing on the scenery of the early life of our Lord; but where the angel met Mary, or where the lowly house of the carpenter stood, no researches can discover.

And with regard to the Transfiguration, might we not still more expect this to be the case? Among all the incidents of Gospel history, none have less of a local character than this. It is a fragment of the eternal light breaking in on the darkness of time; and whether the apostles had been rapt, like Paul, into the third heaven to behold it, or had seen it on this earth, would seem of comparatively little moment. It is the unseen world becoming for a brief interval seen, and proving that the unseen is not necessarily invisible. The persons in the scene are gathered from the depths of the invisible world, "whether in the body or out of the body we cannot tell." The scenery was not Tabor or Hermon, or any sweep of earthly landscape, or snowy heights of mountain solitude; but night and an overshadowing cloud. That cloud wrapped those within it as effectually from earth as if it had been millions of miles of planetary distance in the furthest heavens. Beyond it was the sleeping world, invisible, and night. Within it were three messengers from the dead, and the Son of God, and day;—the day of heaven beaming from the face of Jesus as the Sun, and glistening on his raiment whiter than snow; and from the cloud a voice, "This is my beloved Son, hear him." The light, and the voice, and the persons were of heaven, not of earth. It is only on the next day, when they went down the hill, that earth meets us again, with its perplexities and necessities, in the questioning Scribes, the wondering crowd which ran to meet the Saviour, the possessed dumb child he healed, and the poor, bewildered, agonized father, whose tearful, fearful prayer he heard. Locality is, indeed, of less importance to a vivid conception of the narrative of the Transfiguration than to that of any other in the New Testament. Whether the cloud of glory rested on Hermon or on Tabor, or on the holy city whose foundations are precious stones and her gates pearl, would make no alteration in the scene. Those who were eye-witnesses of that majesty and listeners to that voice were blind and deaf for the time to all earthly sights and sounds; as we shall be when once more that glory is unveiled, and the momentary radiance of the Transfiguration shall fade into the permanent light of the glorious Epiphany of the Son of God.

Through the afternoon, after descending Tabor, we rode across the sultry table-land, longing for water, for on Tabor we had not come on any spring. The country becomes volcanic in character from the base of Tabor eastward to Tiberias. In many parts the plain was thickly strewn with large, black, rounded stones. At an hour or two from the base of Tabor we reached a village, with a large rocky threshing floor, where men were working. We hoped to have found water here, but the villagers directed us further on to their well, which, they said, was at some distance. Whether we missed this well of theirs or not, I cannot tell; but the first water we reached was a spring at the bottom of a black, volcanic, ravine cliff, in the plain, which had so bitter, bituminous a taste, that neither we nor our horses could drink of it. We scrambled out of the ravine, therefore, as soon as possible, and made all haste across the rest of the table-land which lay between us and the basin of Tiberias. When we arrived at the edge of this reach of the deep volcanic ghor or Jordan valley, the lake lay rippling and sparkling, a broad expanse of refreshing waters, some hundred feet below us. We had difficulty in restraining the eagerness of our thirsty horses, as they hurried down the stony hill to this paradise of waters. I forgot at the moment that this lake was indeed fresh, and not salt and bitter like the Dead Sea, and was mournfully anticipating the disappointment which awaited the poor, eager horses, when to my delight, on reaching the brink of the lake, they rushed into the water, and plunged their heads into it, and drank with most unquestionable enjoyment.

The luxury of this sea—these exhaustless miles of fresh and wholesome water, good for drinking or bathing—after husbanding a cup full of the same precious liquid in our hot pitchers all the day, is not easily described. No wonder so many cities flourished on its shores.

We descended to the lake close to the walls of Tiberias, which leant with the concussion of the earthquake which laid it waste in 1837. Our thirsty horses had left us little leisure to linger over our first view of the lake, as it burst on us from the edge of the hill,—once a busy scene of life and labor and traffic, bright with cities and boats, now a lonely mountain lake—reflected in its unbroken waters the white walls of only one poor tottering town, and bearing on its bosom only one poor crazy boat. The road to the Baths, where our tents were pitched, lay close to the lake, over shingly beaches; with black volcanic stones and ruins of the old Roman Tiberias, strewn here and there on our right, over the little level space between the water and the hills, or rather the steep sides of the plain.

Our encampment was close to the Hot Spring, on the shingle between the Bath House and the lake; and here we were to be at home for two whole days and three nights, from this Friday evening till Monday morning. The thought was rest and delight indeed.

The heat on those June days was intense, of that sultry, steady, tropical kind which we had experienced at the Dead Sea; and, with the exception of one morning's ride, the hardiest amongst us could do little else than rest, and look, and stroll after sunset along the beach. Nor did we desire much else. The sites of the cities around the Lake of Tiberias are so much disputed that its interest lies in the general character of the scenery far more than in especial spots; and since we could not visit every nook and corner as we had wished, the next best thing was to have leisure to drink in the scenery and associations of the lake in one characteristic part of it, which we did. By day we rested in the room belonging to the Baths, built by Ibrahim Pasha, the large windows of which, when we could venture to open the Venetians, give us a full view of the lake. Our tents would have been quite unendurable during the heat of the day. Indeed, the lake itself was the only pleasant place during the hottest hours, and in it the gentlemen of our party spent much of their time.

Beyond the Baths the hot sulphurous springs, which, since the days of Herod, have made this place famous, trickled over the pebbles into the lake, throwing out a strong sulphurous smell.

On Saturday morning (June 28th,) we breakfasted outside our tents before the sun rose, and watched the grey and then the glow of dawn spread over the hills "on the other side;" the hills among which the demonaic once roamed, and where the cave tombs, where he abode, still honeycomb the ravines. We were told we must on no account venture to cross to those hills, on account of the savage predatory habits of the Bedouins who infest them. The solitary boat which floats on the lake did not appear during our stay; but, if it had been within reach, we were warned by no means to attempt a voyage in it, because in the sudden storms of wind which burst on this inland sea, as of old, she becomes unmanageable by the unskilful boatmen, and has been detained for days on the opposite shores, involving serious peril from the robber hordes.

Our horses were ready very early, and we started for an exploration of the shores. Crossing the shingly beach again, and passing the ruins of the old city, we rode under the walls of Tiberias, and then skirted the hills which, beyond it, descend precipitously into the lake, on a road hewn in their rocky sides —a Roman road probably, we thought, for since Roman days, since New Testament days, since the fall of Herod's dynasty, what roadmakers have been here? What cities are there now, since Chorazin and Bethsaida fell into nameless heaps, between which any such communication is needed? The poor Jews of Tiberias have no merchandise to convey along these shores, and except a peasant's mule, laden with corn from the plain of Gennesaret, or a stray Bedouin horseman, who scorns or dreads all highways, what feet now tread these paths, so carefully and laboriously cut out of the black volcanic cliffs into a road, in some places wide enough for two chariots to pass? Therefore, we concluded we were, in this rock-hewn road, on the sure track of Him who went about this lake doing good, from Capernaum to Bethsaida and Chorazin; and the thought made us ride in silence.

Beyond those cliffs the hills retreat, and the shores of the lake widen into an extensive fertile plain, watered by many streams. This, we were told, was Gennesaret; and before we reached it the road diverged a little, leaving room for a height of volcanic rock between us and the lake, crowned with the black ruins of a building, with a few huts near it, called, in accents scarcely changed since Mary Magdalene dwelt there, Mejdel. On these rocky shores she wandered distracted by the terrible reality of the demoniac voices, wilder than the wildest dreams of madness, and yet, alas! no dreams. On these shores, probably, she first heard the voice which hushed the tempest in her soul, with its unfailing "Peace, be still!" And hither, we may suppose, she returned after the resurrection, the first witness of the risen Lord, with his "Mary" awaiting the response of "Raboni" in her heart for ever.

The locality of the plain of Gennesaret is disputed; some authorities placing it on this plain near Tiberias, and others on the low fertile lands near the flowing of the Jordan into the lake on the north. The scenery of either would correspond with that of the Galilean parable of the sower and the seed, which naturally, not having seen the other, we now associate with the rich plain we crossed on that morning's ride.

Here were the hills sweeping down the "stony ground" into the fertile soil of the plain. Here was the way-side, now indeed little trodden; and here were the fowls of the air. Birds abound round the shores of the lake, not merely the doves and wood-pigeons which coo and murmur in the groves throughout Palestine, but birds of various kinds, and among others, birds of prey; we had seen eagles hovering and wheeling over the bare cliffs. Thorns and prickly bushes abound everywhere in Palestine. And here certainly was abundance of the good ground which could bring forth some forty, some sixty, some an hundred fold.

Along this fruitful plain we rode for a long time between the lake and the cultivated land, pacing leisurely over the sandy beaches which border this part of the lake, the little waves rippling up and bathing our horses' feet, and shrubberies of oleanders in full flower leaning towards us on the other side. Every now and then the beaches widened into little sandy coves, through which little pebbly brooks trickled into the lake; and once or twice we had to wade through the mouths of deeper streams.

There was something indescribably happy in thus leisurely riding along the shores of that sacred lake, as we thought what voice the music of its soft ripples had once accompained, and whose feet its waves had bathed. At the end of this reach of the lake, this bay of rich, low, level land, we came to a ruinous khan, called Khan Minyeh.

The best kept of khans have a dreary deserted look to European eyes, unconsciously comparing them with inns and their welcomes. A quadrangle of bare roughly built sheds around a desolate court-yard, constitute their highest attractions; but Kahn Minyeh was a ruined kahn, and around it, as so often in this land of the "desolation of many generations," were scattered ruins of an earlier date. We left our horses near it and climbed a hill just above, which commanded a fine view of the lake. We were told that the ruins on its brow were those of Capernaum; but be this as it may, they were almost certainly the ruins of a city in whose streets the Saviour taught, under whose roofs he rested, and at whose gates he healed the sick.

At the time we were there we thought ourselves actually on the site of the city which was so habitually the resting-place of our Lord when near the Sea of Galilee, that it is called his own city.

The lake lay before us in nearly its whole extent from south to north, point stretching beyond point into pale distance. The shores were for the most part steep, but not mountainous, and the outline of the hills not much varied. There was scarcely anything with sufficient form left in it to be called ruins. Indeed, we might have fancied the black unshapen stones strewn around us to have been rather the *débris* of some volcanic convulsion than the remains of human dwellings. In one place, however, there was a deep pit or broken cistern, and near it lay a large stone with a circle engraven on it, like a millstone or press of some kind. The thin grass was dried to an amber brown by the intense summer heat, and the dry stalks and withered ears waved languidly in the breeze.

Yet here, we thought, had been the home of Jairus, where the only child had died, and had been recalled again to life by the voice which called the dead from Hades with such tender quiet words, as those with which the mother would have waked her from sleep, "Talitha (little maiden, a term of endearment), I say unto thee, Arise." And in the streets once standing here the trembling woman had touched the hem of his garment and had been healed.

Here the centurion, whose servant was dear unto him, had lived, and the nobleman, courtier perhaps of Herod, who found his fever-stricken son healed by the distant word he had not heard; and here, in consequence of that miracle, sprang up at least one believing household.

And here the city was once at sunset emptied of its inhabitants, empty as it is now, for every house sent forth all its inmates, "sick and whole," thronging to the gate where Jesus stood and healed all who had need of healing. Fancy the tears and smiles and broken words of gratitude and joy as the multitude returned to homes from which, for the time at least, all suffering and pain were banished. Pain—but not sin! The words which once sounded over those waves as a fearful warning, "Thou, Capernaum, which art exalted to heaven, shall be cast down to hell, for if the mighty works done in thee had been done in Sodom it would have remained," were unheeded, and they have become a wail of doom which echoes from every point and hillside of these deserted and lonely shores. They were no solitude then. The white columns of temples and palaces and synagogues, and the sails of countless boats, gleamed over land and sea, and were reflected in these still waters. Busy, trading cities, baths which were the luxurious resorts of Herod's court, stimulated the energies of husbandman, fisherman, and merchant. And those plains below us, if they were indeed the corn-fields through which the disciples walked and plucked the ears of corn, were no unfrequented paths. Our Lord came that the world through him might be saved, and wherever men thronged most thickly lay his path. The busy, peopled, cultivated shores of the Lake of Geneva might perhaps give us some idea of what the lake of Tiberias was.

Yet always as now the desert plains must on these shores have trenched close on the peopled cities. The barren black volcanic hills which in many places rise precipitously from the lake, must always have been solitary and uncultivated.

One of our party rode further and saw the ruins of the white columns of a temple, contrasting strangely with the black stones of most of the ruinous heaps in this district. In some of the hills were quarries of white marble, which, no doubt, rang in New Testament days with the blows of the workmen. But we were warned not to venture further in the heat of the day, and therefore slowly retraced our steps by sandy coves and shingly beaches, gathering the beautiful rose-colored flowers of the oleanders among their fresh green leaves—fresh as if no sun could scorch them:—traversing again the rock-hewn road on the cliff, and passing Tiberias to our tents by the baths.

All that day we could do little but rest and bathe. The bathroom behind the hall, which contained the divan which we appropriated, was built by Ibrahim Pasha. It had a stone roof supported on handsome marble columns, taken from the ruins of the old Roman Tiberias, close at hand. Here all the men bathed together. Opening into this was a little room with a bath intended, we were told, to wash the feet in, when the bathers came from the soil-covered floor of the great bath. It was a vivid illustration of the words, "He that is washed needeth not save to wash his feet."

In the evening when the sun was set, we ventured out for a little stroll towards the Roman ruins on one side, and across the hot springs on the other, round a little quiet creek through which they flow. But the heat even then and throughout the night was very great. It was long before the black volcanic rocks would cool in that hollow furnace of the Jordan valley, which at Tiberias is three hundred feet below the level of the Mediterranean.

The next day (Sunday) was one of especial enjoyment. The heat of the day combined to make rest desirable, and no further explorations of the regions round about could have been more interesting than simply sitting

Tiberias and the Sea of Galilee.

p. 321.

still and watching the changes of light and shade over lake and hill, with the Bible in our hands.

We sat on the divan in the bath house, which had windows on three sides with Venetian blinds, these we kept open on the shady side, thus changing the view as the sun went round.

On the north we looked towards Tiberias, whose white walls and towers leant from the point they fortify towards the lake, and were reflected in it. On the right of these stretched the broad sweep of sparkling sea, with long smooth lines crossing it, here and there marking the currents, and bounded by the hilly shores, distance beyond distance, in some places separated from the water by a narrow strip of sand, whilst beyond and above all towered the distant range of Lebanon and Hermon streaked with snow. Between us and Tiberias the narrow beach was strewn with large black stones, the relics of the Roman town, mingled with the rocks swept down from the steep cliffs which hemmed it in.

On the south the shores curved more rapidly, enclosing the waters in a smaller circle. The little shingly creek through which the hot springs trickled from their source in the abrupt cliff a few yards behind the baths was bounded by a cluster of ruinous Turkish-looking buildings, whose domes were relieved against the paler hills on the "other side."

Immediately opposite us the hills seemed to rise abruptly from the lake with no intervening strip of sand; and although they were said to be five miles distant, it was difficult to believe it, so distinctly were every bright projecting point and brake relieved against each other on the sky, and so plainly were each dark ravine and cleft defined. All day they glowed in the intense heat as in the blaze of an open furnace, and the hot golden tints were reflected far into the still lake,—each fiery peak and purple cleft as clear there as above; the reflection only divided from the reality by a long broad line of intensely blue water in the distance, at the base of the cliffs. All through the sultry noon, lake and hilly shores lay before us in one dazzling haze of fiery light.

Then a light breeze sprang up, and came towards us from the east, marking its path across the lake by a line of ripple, and at last breaking the little waves on the pebbles at our feet with a cool music.

When the sun had set, we crept out of our shelter, and strolled again over the shingly beach, picking up a few rounded pebbles, or tiny fresh-water shells, and watching the countless fish dart about under the clear water, or spring from it. Then we sat down on some of the black stones strewn over the beach, enjoying the breeze, with all the gospel narratives we had been reading about the Sea of Galilee and its coast in our hearts. And henceforth the old familiar names rise before us new and vivid pictures.

On this shingle or near it the apostles' nets had been stretched to dry.

At the point where we were encamped, the beach sloped so abruptly into the lake that a few steps into the water would take any one out of his depth. It must have been in just such a place that Peter's boat was thrust out a little from the land. A few feet would have been enough to place the boat beyond the reach of the eager crowd, so that every syllable of those "words of everlasting life" might have been distinctly audible to every one of the multitude compressed on this narrow beach between the cliffs and the lake.

It would be impossible to gather a great multitude on these shores now. Cities, ships—all are gone! No tolls to be gathered now on these deserted shores;—no fishing boats ply among the countless fish in the lake. Now and then a couple of wild Bedouin horsemen would pass by us, straying from their haunts on the other side, which are so perilously near as to make a guard necessary for us at night. Now and then, a pair of white veiled women came with pitchers to the hot springs, or a family of depressed looking Jews would rest in the shade of the baths, on their way to Tiberias, which is one of their sacred cities. But the silence and desolation of these shores are oppressive. It is remarkable that Tiberias, a city not once mentioned in the gospels as the scene of our Lord's teaching or miracles, is the only one left on the lake.

But the time of deepest enjoyment to us was the late evening, when no stray traveller could venture out, and nothing was heard but the trickling of the hot springs over the shingle, and the cool splashing of the little waves upon the beach.

Then we could imagine the sudden rush of the storm down the ravines of those steep shores on the lake, the helpless tossing of the fishing-boat on the convulsed and foaming waters, the majestic tread of a human form on the billows, the calm words of command from a human voice instantly hushing the winds and smoothing the waves into such a calm as that around us now.

That human form we felt is in heaven now, that divine presence is around us still, that human voice we shall indeed hear. And as we sat on the brink of the lake, which had so long been to us like an allegory of life, and bathed our hands in the cool waves, all the quiet night seemed full of the words which once floated across these waters, "Be of good cheer, it is I, be not afraid;" and all our hearts seemed full of the response which broke once from the apostles' lips, "Truly this is the Son of God."

Yet one scene was perhaps more present with us than any other throughout that Sunday,—and especially at each of the three sunrises we saw over the lake,—the scene which almost more vividly and familiarly than any other brings before us our risen Saviour, the first fruits in whose likenesses all that sleep in Him shall be raised.

It was the time when Jesus showed himself again to the disciples by the Sea of Tiberias,—that last supplementary chapter of St. John's Gospel, which seems to lead us beyond the grave to the shores of life on "the other side," and yet whose chief delight it is that its scene was here on this actual, familiar, untransformed earth, on one of these very sandy or shingly beaches. We could not but recall continually the solitary figure seem dimly from the boat after the night of toil and disappointment in the grey of the morning; the voice recognised at last by its power in the repetition of the old miracle; old, yet new in the significant variety of the safe landing of the unbroken net with all its contents at the feet of Jesus; the simple meal which the Master provided from his stores, not from theirs; and afterwards, more than all, the familiar converse as the little band, "when they had dined," walked along this shore.

Yes, along this shore; with the quiet music of these waters rippling against the beach, and the golden outlines of the opposite hills reflected on the lake in the early morning, that little band walked on, conversing as they went; and before them the risen

Lord, the One who had died, was alive again, and would die no more, speaking, as he walked, to Peter in few and quiet words which went to the depths of the heart. The past threefold denial, recalled by the threefold question, but only recalled to stamp a deeper consecration on the service of the future. This was the scene which, more than any other, seemed before us.

The fire of charcoal smouldering on this beach to welcome the weary fishermen; the fishes laid thereon, and the flat unleavened cakes (such as were often prepared for us) baked on the ashes; the Lord himself taking the bread and fish and giving them to the disciples; and after the simple meal the quiet conversation as they walked along the shore, —and then the gleams of allegoric meaning which flash through all these homely details, lifting the heart to the heavenly shore; and the net which, "when it is full," the angels shall come forth and lay at the feet of Jesus, no more treading the stormy sea, or tossed in the frail boat, but standing in majesty on the eternal shore. And afterwards the "feast," — not a morning meal then, but a "supper," an evening feast when the long day of toil is over, and when the "Lovest thou me?" shall be exchanged for the "In that thou didst it unto me;" and the "Feed my sheep" for "Well done, good and faithful servant, thou hast been faithful in a few things, I will make thee ruler over many things; enter thou into the joy of thy Lord."

Thus if through the night the Sea of Galilee seems to echo with the heart-calming assurance, "It is I, be not afraid," its shores at morning seem no less to resound with the heart-stirring question, "Lovest thou me?"

And for all the nights and mornings of life, what sweeter and stronger words can cheer and brace the heart than these, spoken by the same voice, to heart after heart, age after age?

XIV.

Galilee.

ON Monday, June the 30th, our sojourn at Tiberias was to close. Once more before mounting our horses, we walked over the places in the immediate neighborhood of the baths, which had grown so familiar to us. The hot springs, steaming with their sulphurous odor as they poured into the lake over the shingly beach; the black stones and rocks scattered round; the little waves curving round our creek; the steep cliffs behind, their slopes tufted here and there with dry, thin vegetation. We gathered a few pebbles and shells, sat a few moments on the rocks, and listened to the ripple of the quiet waves —drew the sweet, fresh water from the lake in the hollow of our hands, and drank, and bathed our faces in it; and brought every sense into contact with the sacred scene, as if instinctively to stamp its reality on our hearts, and to associate a recollection with every sense, when memory and pictures would be all we had left of it.

We had seen the lake in so many aspects. At midnight we had looked out from our tent door, quite close to the water's edge, over the clear sky, full of brilliant stars and countless nebulæ, with one planet shining over the dim hills on the other side, and casting a long silvery reflection like moonlight on the rippling lake. At early morn we had watched the glorious golden dawn spread over the sky above the eastern hills, till the sun rose behind them; in the haze of noonday heat we had seen it with the reflection of the opposite mountains warm and rich, and every crevice and cove distinct in the reality and the reflection; with the breeze rippling the waters, and crisping the little waves into foam, and so still that the fish could be seen swimming through it in multitudes, their leaping up the only sound which broke the silence. We had been by its deserted cities, its gardens or wildernesses of oleanders in full rosy bloom; its quiet sands and pebbly beaches; its black, volcanic, craggy hills, and "desert places near the cities;" and now we were to travel for a few days through Galilee of the Gentiles.

We soon climbed the shoulder of the height above Tiberias, and reached the hill with two summits or horns on the edge of the table-land, from which we had our last near, yet comprehensive view of the lake. This hill is called Kurun Hattin, and is entitled by tradition the Mount of Beatitudes—those who have studied the subject seem to think with every probability of truth. It is a mountain—a distinct and elevated summit—and yet not wild and craggy, but containing platforms and slopes on which multitudes might have gathered and listened. Its situation is central; great multitudes from the towns and villages among the wooded hills of Galilee on the north, from Decapolis, even from Jerusalem, and from beyond Jordan, might easily congregate here—whilst Capernaum, into which our Lord entered so shortly after the sermon on the mount, and healed the centurion's servant, is [if the site be near Khan Minyeh] quite close at hand on the shore below.

There is something in the commanding situation of Kurun Hattin peculiarly suitable for a discourse spoken "with authority." The sermon on the mount is so different in character from most of our Lord's teaching. It is not so much the Oriental teacher, the Rabbi, impressing truths on disciples with endless variety of parable and illustration. Still less is it the friend conversing with friend, as on the quiet beaches of Gennesaret. It is the Lawgiver, the royal Lawgiver, proclaiming from the throne the laws of the kingdom of God—the laws by which he will judge when he sits on the judgment seat. And this hill, commanding the wide plain of Hattin, and, far below, the blue waters of the Sea of Galilee in their deep, oval hollow, (then reflecting in its bosom the white walls of busy cities, and the marble facades of Roman villas, and the sunlit or tawny sails of countless boats,) seems a fit throne for such a proclamation.

It began not judicially, but divinely ; not with denunciations, but with benedictions ; and then through all its searching and humbling, yet homely precepts, sealed by the majestic "I say unto you," it proceeds to the announcement of that day when the most appalling words that can be heard will be those from his lips, "I never knew you ; depart from me, ye that work iniquity." The benedictions were unheeded, the promises were disregarded, the warnings were despised ; and now on that house of prosperity and splendor, "built on the sand," the "rain" has indeed "descended," and the winds have blown, and it has fallen, and "great has been the fall of it."

The gracious title, Mount of Beatitudes, echoes with a reproachful tenderness, sadder than any curse from that height on the do serted shores of the forsaken, lonely Sea of Galilee.

With the recommencing of our journey, recommenced one of the most continually interesting features of our sojourn in the Holy Land—the realizing in some measure, by our own toil and fatigue, what the toil and weariness of our Lord must have been during the ceaseless journeys on foot of the years of his ministry, so much of which was spent in Galilee. Galilee is not an easy country to travel over in this hot climate. It is very hilly; and it is impossible to pass from one village to another on these hillsides, or among these narrow valleys, without climbing many a steep and rugged path.

After leaving Kurun Hattin we crossed a ridge of hills, partly wooded with evergreen trees and shrubs, with prickly or glossy leaves, into another plain, or low broad valley, parched and waterless. Here, we had been told, was one of the supposed sites of Cana of Galilee; but our guide, through some misunderstanding, had been left behind, and therefore we had to trust to our own researches.

The soil of the valley seemed fertile, and in some places cultivated; but the crops had all been gathered in, and we had to plough our way through the dry clods of brown, sun-baked earth, among which from time to time were scattered round stones like potatoes, which, when broken, we found contained crystals of spar in the centre.

Hills more or less wooded swept down into the valley, and on the sides of these we often saw ruins, which we thought might be those of Cana, and were sure must be those of towns and villages where our Lord taught and healed the sick on his many journeys to teach and preach in their cities. We rode up the hill-sides to two of these heaps of ruins. Their extent, and the size of the carefully hewn stones, gave them more claim to the title of cities than to that of mere villages. In both there were a number of ruined walls, not merely scattered stones, as in the poor ruins of Southern Palestine, but fragments of well-built, massive walls, with extensive water-tanks and deep wells, now, indeed, all dry. At the second there was a very fine deep well, with a large carved trough beside it, all now dry and empty, and full of snakes crawling up its sides. We should have examined this more closely, but for a skirmish among our horses, one of which was vicious, and in his efforts to bite another, nearly wounded one of us, but happily only tore the clothes instead. Nevertheless, we had time to speculate whether this well, now so significantly haunted by serpents and noisome reptiles, was not once the pure and abundant fountain from which were filled the six water-pots of stone at the marriage-feast. No vineyards now on these slopes, no water in these fountains to be turned into wine by miracle, or by the wondrous chemistry of nature, meekly ministering always at the command of the same voice; no festive homes now in the village, where Jesus, and his mother, and his disciples once were guests!

On descending the hill we had to ride still a long way through the hot valley, without shade, or water, or refreshment of any kind (our muleteer with the provision saddle-bags having failed us), until we came to a village. It was a dreary, oppressive ride along that burning plain or valley, where the hills kept off all the air, but gave no shade. From sunrise when we started, till past noon, through out that valley, we saw not one human being, and tasted not one drop of water but the cupful we had brought in our little flasks. This is perhaps partly the reason why the village we reached on that noon, (the name of which we do not know) stands out as such a cool, refreshing picture, a green type of shade, and refreshment, and rest. It was situated on a slope at the further end of the plain. The oxen were treading out the corn on the threshing-floor levelled in the rocky side of the hill, and near it was a spring of good, cool, sweet water, an abundance of which was poured into the troughs for our thirsty horses. It was always one of the especial pleasures of our journey to see and hear the eager delight with which those tired, patient creatures sucked the water when we came to a well.

The people of this village were very friendly and open-hearted. When we dismounted they brought us bread and water, and what was a rare luxury, an abundant supply of good sweet milk.

Our horses were fastened to the outer branches of a gigantic oak, whilst we rested under the shade of the same tree; and the villagers assembled in various groups around us, the men gravely sitting on the ground in little parties, discussing the strangers, and the women timidly approaching in the background, wondering especially at the Frank "sit" (lady).

In many of the villages through which we passed it would neither have been pleasant nor safe thus to dismount and repose without guard or arms of any kind in the midst or the people. More than once angry and contemptuous glances and gestures had been directed against us, which made us glad to escape; but in this Galilean village all seemed simple, and friendly, and hospitable, reminding one of the tales of Arab simplicity and hospitality scattered through French "Recueils choisis," and juvenile literature of that kind.

Thus we had a delicious hour of repose and refreshment under the shade of that magnificent oak, with the hum of the villagers' conversation lulling us to sleep, like the noon-day murmur of bees. But there was one little incident in connection with that friendly village which more than all its shade, and hospitality, has stamped it with a kind of tender, sacred interest in our memories.

Among many of these simple peasants there is a prevalent belief that every Frank is a Hakim, a wise man, a doctor, a physician. Before we left, therefore, two or three of the women who had been timidly hovering near, ventured close, and taking me as the mediator, anxiously pointing to the sick children in their arms. The little creatures were evidently drooping and suffering. One poor mother I especially remember who brought us two sick little ones, and seemed to forget all her timidity in her longing to have them cured, and her confidence that we could do them good. We can never forget her imploring looks and gestures, and the beseeching tones of her voice, as she looked at us and then pointed to the little sufferers. And we could only stroke the little drooping head that leaned languidly on her bosom, and take the little feverish hands in ours, and give her kind looks, and hoping she would understand the pity in our tones, as well as we could not fail to comprehend the distress in hers.

She little knew the mingled emotions her entreaties called up in our hearts, or the scenes they recalled of the days of the Son of man on earth, when in this Galilee, perhaps in this very village, they "brought unto Him all that were diseased, and he healed them." "For in Him was life," and in us was nothing to help these poor, distressed, confiding people! It touched us very deeply to be appealed to in this way as superior beings, and feel so powerless to do or even to say anything to help them. How we longed to tell those poor mothers of Him!

But kind looks and a little money were all we had to give these friendly villagers, and with many a lingering look we mounted our horses and took leave of our hosts.

From this village the scenery became less monotonous and dreary. We left the burning narrow plain along which we had been riding so many hours, and crossed some beautiful breezy hills, wooded with green shrubs, dwarf trees, like a coppice lately felled, with some of the taller trees left standing. On the other side of the hills we came to a large village called Shef Arma, where the women crowded round me with eager childish curiosity, wanting to examine the contents of my carriage bag, and the meaning of my note book, which I took out and wrote in to amuse them. We had to wait here some little time to gain information as to our tents, which we found had been pitched at the further end of the town. We were not sorry to escape from the curious crowds who were rapidly gathering around us. They were by no means so respectful and courteous in their demeanor as the friendly peasants in the village of our midday halt, and we were glad to find our encampment removed some little way from the houses in an olive garden at the outskirts of the town. Near our tents was a large draw-well, at which the women of the village seemed incessantly to be filling their pitchers. The veiled figures were constantly passing with pitchers on their heads or shoulders, and the noise of eager talking, broken every now and then by angry disputing, did not cease till sunset, and recommenced before sunrise the next morning.

On Tuesday, July the 1st, we set off soon after sunrise for Caipha on the sea coast, and Carmel. Our route, after descending from the hills, lay over sand heaps covered with dry, long-stalked plants, varied with flowering shrubs, one with a crimson bell-shaped flower, and another with blue spike of blossom like the Veronica in our gardens. It reminded me of the sands swept in for miles by the Atlantic on some parts of the western coast of Cornwall, tossed by waves, and drifted by winds into countless hillocks, bound together by coarse grass and various seaside plants.

On our left rose the range of Carmel, which we were approaching, and which forms the point at the southern extremity of the bay. Some of our party diverged from the plain, and rode a little way along its wooded sides. Carmel is not an isolated height like Tabor, or even a distinct mountain like Hermon, but a long range of fertile hills broken by wooded dells, yet sufficiently united to constitute one ridge, terminating in the steep cliffs of the promontory, from which the white walls of the great mother-convent of the Carmelites look far over the Mediterranean. Among that long wooded range was the rocky height in the forest, commanding sea and plain, with its spring near it, which is supposed to be the scene of Elijah's sacrifice. But of this we did not hear until too late to visit it.

Before reaching Caipha, at the foot of the promontory, we forded a wide but shallow stream, close to the sea. We were told to follow carefully and closely in the steps of our guide, because, above and below, the current was stronger and deeper, and might cause us some difficulty. Where we crossed it did not wet our feet, and just served to cool the legs of our horses. Yet this was "that ancient river—the river Kishon," which forces its way through a pass of Carmel some few miles above. Its whole course in summer is not more than a few miles, and its depth, I believe, in no part sufficient to navigate the smallest boats. But it is perennial, a quality which gives any stream, of a few miles' course, a claim to be called "ancient," in the land of the shortlived summer torrents; and after the rains, no doubt it would sweep a fugitive army, attempting to cross it without knowing the fords, with irresistible force into the sea. More than this the song of Deborah does not imply, although to the northern imaginations the words certainly suggest a very different river, from the small stream quietly pursuing its way over the sands which we forded on that summer noon.

In Caipha we watered our horses. It was more like a town than any place we had entered since leaving Jerusalem, but not one Bible association detained us among its narrow streets, and after a short delay, we commenced the ascent to the promontory of Carmel. The road was good and wound up the face of the hill, overlooking the sea, and in some places shaded by fine trees.

In the convent we were most kindly and hospitably entertained by Frère Charles, who had just returned from a tour on the business of his order in France. He showed us his album, to which all visitors, if they wish it, are desired to contribute either with pen or pencil. The air of the whole place was rather French than Oriental, from our polite and lively entertainer himself, to the suite of rooms with French furniture provided for those who wish to stay any time at the convent. There was certainly little in what we saw there to recall either Elijah, according to Carmelite tradition, the founder of the order, or St. Louis, the founder of this convent; but into the interior of the monastery, of course, feminine feet dare not intrude. From the windows, and from the garden below, we looked down on the Mediterranean, breaking on the sands at the foot of Carmel far below. The steep sides of the cliff were dotted with olives, and with the breezes on this height, this broad sweep of sea in front, and the fruitful wooded range of Mount Carmel, with its glades and shady dells stretching inland behind, one can well fancy a heart weary with the hollow conventionalities of the European world turning to the monastic seclusion of this mountain, swept clear of conventionalities (it might be fancied) by the grand recollections of its solitary prospect, as its atmosphere is swept pure of malaria by the sea-breezes. There are, moreover, means of exercising benevolence in the Pharmacie, now presided over by an Italian monk. We understood Frère Charles to say that many of the neighboring peasants apply for medical advice and remedies here, but that little gratitude is manifested by them, and no missionary work making progress among them. Have any of the monks who reside here, and say mass over "Elijah's cave," indeed come here with such thoughts, and if so, what have they found? Rest for those heavy-laden with earth's cares—reality and truth for those weary with the world's falsehood—are to be found in no *place* or *thing*, but in One Person, as near us in Paris as on Carmel. It would be interesting to know something of these Syrian convents, whose outer courts make such hospitable resting-places for travellers,—unless, indeed, the monastery is only the reproduction of the hollow outside world in miniature, the larger ambitions of the court and camp exchanged for the petty ambitions of the monk.

With a grateful feeling toward Frère Charles for his cheerful courtesy, we left the convent in the afternoon, and wound our way again down the face of the cliff to Caipha.

From Caipha, after recrossing the Kishon, we had a beautiful cool ride of fifteen miles, over the sands along the curve of the bay of Akka (Acre). Here our encampment was in a garden, or orchard of palms, figs, and olives. Our Maltese cook had established his crocks and pans under the romantic shade of those trees. A little stream or river crept quietly along beside our garden, and found its way into the sea over the sands, not five minutes' walk off. The murmur of the Mediterranean made music for us all day and night. In sight rose the walls and towers of Acre, with all its crusading memories. Altogether it was a kind of "pleasant arbor" in the "Hill Difficulty" of our material pilgrimage, and the spirit of dreaminess and slumber came over us, so that between that and a discussion as to our future route, we did not leave our garden until rather late in the next day, Wednesday, July the 22d.

In the afternoon we rode through the poor streets and bazaars of Acre, and then leaving it, along the undulating sand-heaps drifted in by the sea to El-Bussah. The views on this reach of the Mediterranean were very fine. A noble amphitheatre enclosed the plain of Acre, from Carmel to the range south of Tyre, an arc of which the blue sea was a chord. At El-Bussah we found an abundant pure spring, rising pure and fresh, as many springs do along the coast from this to Tyre, within a few yards of the sea. Cattle were being watered there; not sheep and goats, "lesser cattle" merely. We did not encamp near the spring, on account of the mosquitoes, but a little further inland, and higher up, beneath the hills which form the great barrier between the Holy Land and the shores of Tyre and Sidon, dividing the maritime plain of the south from that of the north.

No sandy beach lies between the sea and this promontory, as at Carmel. To cross from the land of Israel to that of the Phœnicians, you must scale the cliff by the rugged path called the Tyrian ladder.

We used the little light left in wandering about the rocky shore, so different from the smooth sands which all along the ancient Philistine coast border the almost tideless Mediterranean. Here on each side of the strip of sand through which the fresh waters of our spring found their way into the sea, stretched a rugged platform of rocks, broken by little salt-water pools, reminding us of those on the coast of Cornwall. Some of our party found shells on the rocks. This is the commencement of the bold high promontory which forms the boundary of Palestine.

The next day (Thursday, July the 23d), was a day of adventures, of some danger and great fatigue; but we cannot regret it, as it gave us a far more extensive acquaintance with the hills and valleys of Galilee, than we should have gained by the ordinary route.

By a misunderstanding, our party was broken into three divisions, one of us wandering off alone, the muleteers, guides, and dragoman taking the ordinary route, whilst four of us, including a German servant, whose stock of Arabic was only a few words richer than our own, set off together expecting to be soon rejoined by the dragoman who had gone in search of our lost companion.

The original goal of the day's march had been Banias, but the muleteers positively pronounced this unattainable ; and the point finally fixed on to be reached was Bint-y-Jebail (the daughter of the mountains), a vilvage deep among the wild hills of Galilee. The name of this village, and its direction by the compass, was all we had to direct us, except that we wished to see, on our way, the ruined castle of Tirschiha, which we had been particularly desired at Jerusalem not to miss.

We first ascended a hill on the right of the plain by El-Bussah, from which we had a beautiful view of the plain of Acre, bounded on the south by Carmel stretching its hilly range far into the sea. On this hill we found a village. It was very silent; it seemed as if the inhabitants had deserted it to work in the fields. But two men appeared in answer to our call, and of them we asked the way to Tirschiha. They pointed across the plain to the opposite hills, but as they spoke they drew so suspiciously near, laying hold of our bridles and looking so dangerous that we were glad to break from them and descend the hill as rapidly as we could. We had been told that the villagers among these Galilean hills are often very unfriendly and thievish, indeed, little better than bandits, to defenceless travellers, and we had no arms amongst us.

On reaching the plain we rode fast over it, and made a most difficult cross-country ascent of the hills on the other side, over rocks and through thickets of prickly bushes, only guided by cattle tracks, and often losing even these. Once in a glade of the forest we caught sight of a herdsman with a drove of cattle, and called to him to show us the way. But the more we ca led him he wouldn't come. He probably mistook us for Bedouins or Bashi Bazouks, and prudently made all haste out of our reach, hiding himself among the brushwood. With this exception we saw or heard no human being for hours, and after wandering from sunrise till noon over this ridge of wooded hill, we found ourselves on the edge of a dark, narrow ravine. From the bottom of this ravine, far, far below, came to us the sound of a stream eddying and falling among stones, like a Devonshire river. It was like the voice of a friend; and after debating some minutes whether we should attempt to skirt the valley or cross it, we could not resist the voice of the river, but dismounted from our horses, and throwing the bridles over their necks, began the perilously steep and rugged descent, guided partly by a track, made probably by wild cattle, to the stream. We reached the border of the river in safety, and resolved to make our midday halt there.

For half an hour after we gave ourselves up to rest. More we dared not allow ourselves, not knowing how many hours of difficult riding might be before us in this wild country. We took the cold chicken and Arab bread out of Wilhelm's saddlebags, and drank of the pure, cold stream. For our poor horses there was nothing but such herbage or leaves as they could crop from the rocks and bushes; but the powers of endurance of these little Syrian horses are wonderful.

The scene around us was quite different from any of our previous experiences of the Holy Land. We could have imagined ourselves in any wooded mountain district in Europe. The ravine was very deep and narrow, and its sides were clothed with tangled wood. At our feet the cold, pure stream or river tumbled over rocks, or eddied in pools with sandy bottoms. Close beside it opposite us rose the ruins of a

Gothic church, with arched doors and windows, a relic, no doubt, of crusading times. Crowning the opposite height far above us rose the ruins of a massive ancient castle. But what this church and castle are called, to this day we know not. It was enough to give interest to that day's wanderings that we were among the hills of Galilee.

After our brief rest our next anxiety was to find a path out of the ravine on the opposite side. When our German servant believed he had discovered one, we followed him across the river, dismounting on the other side to lead our horses through the prickly thickets, under the branches of the trees, which grew too low to admit of our riding under them. But the path became more and more impracticable, and at last disappeared altogether, blocked up by masses of rock. Two of us went forward, leaving the four horses in charge of the rest, and scrambled with much difficulty up the precipitous rocks, to see if we could anywhere descry a practicable path. By climbing over rocks, rubbish, and ruins, we reached the foot of the castle, and there found again traces of the path the fallen rocks had blocked up. The frightened horses had to be dragged round by the same way, as no other appeared. One of them all but lost his balance on the precipitous rocks, and the others reared and struggled, but at length they were all brought safely through into the clearer space, and we remounted. The castle was very extensive and massive, with ruined walls fallen into the moats. It appeared to us, from the brief investigation we had time to bestow, a fortress of the Crusaders, reared on the gigantic foundations of ancient Phœnician or Hebrew builders. Anything more impressive to the imagination could hardly be seen than these solitary (and to us nameless) ruins of a castle and church rising by this unknown river in the wild woods of Galilee, and yet leading the mind back so plainly to era beyond era of past human history. It was strange to think of the strains of the Te

Deum and the old Church hymns rising from that lowly church in the Galilean valley, and of the old Phœnician fortress echoing back the praises of the Nazarene—the Galilean.

We were thankful to get over this difficulty, which our entire ignorance of the country made really a danger, but this difficulty surmounted left us still in great perplexity. Of the distance to Bint-y-Jebail we had no idea, and the compass, which with the map gave us our only knowledge of the direction in which it lay, was a very imperfect guide in a country seamed with precipitous ravines covered with tangled wood. Soon after leaving the castle our path was crossed by another. I believe prayer for protection and guidance was indeed answered that day, for the danger in that thinly peopled country, where the few villages were inhabited by people we could not safely trust, was not small. Our great anxiety was lest darkness should overtake us in this wilderness, although it would have been safer to bivouac in the forest than to seek the shelter of an unknown village. Meantime the scenery was the finest we had seen in Palestine; ranges of lofty wooded hills, folding over each other, distance beyond distance, as far as the eye could reach from the heights; — not sprinkled with trees in park-like groups like Tabor, but thickly clothed with forest, tangled in many places with an undergrowth of luxuriant brushwood; deep wild ravines, and beautiful woodland paths through forests of evergreen oak and other trees, sweet clematis and wild convolvulus garlanding the trees, and countless other wild flowers springing in every brake and glade. And this was Galilee.

For miles after leaving the castle we did not meet or see one human being, nor even any cattle, or trace of man. When we lost sight of that watered valley, we scrambled over several high ridges, and crossed another magnificent wooded ravine, with a dry watercourse, and spanned by a bridge, near which was an abandoned well. There was something very weird and solemn in these traces of long-past human labor and life amongst these solitudes. At length, however, we came in sight of something like cultivation, and then of an Arab village. Wilhelm asked the way. They said Bint-y-Jebail was five hours off. We inquired again of some people we met in the path, and received contrary information and directions. At the next village a very unfriendly looking peasant, working in the fields, of whom we asked directions, laid hold of one of our bridles, and wanted us to wait until some neighbors, to whom he called, came up, but we thought it imprudent to encounter an assembly of the villagers, and galloped off from him as rapidly as we could across ploughed fields and through low stone walls like Dartmoor hedges, until we came to what seemed more like a beaten track, where a peaceable looking man on a donkey met us and told us the way. Across more hills to another village. Here the men were away in the fields, but two or three women at a well were friendly, gave us water from their pitchers, and said (as we understood) that Bint-y-Jebail was only an hour off. This revived our failing hopes, and we rode off again as rapidly as we could, up and down wooded hills and along valleys for nearly two hours, our agile but tired horses clambering over slabs of rock on the steep hill sides with wonderful perseverance. At length we reached another village in a valley, which, we trusted, must be our destination, but to our dismay here we were told Bint-y-Jebail was three hours further on. The sun, by this time, was not an hour above the horizon; in the valleys twilight began already to creep over the forest, and a wolf had daringly crossed the road in front of us, at a distance of a few yards. One of our party advocated waiting, and trying the hospitality of the villagers; but this was concluded too great a risk. Accordingly, by means of entreaties and a dollar, we persuaded a peasant to guide us across the hills to Bint-y-Jebail. It was a wild ride, and our horses stumbled in the darkness before we reached the village; and when we reached it we looked in vain for our tents; but to our great joy a man met us at the large reservoir—into which our tired horses pressed—at the entrance of the village, and mentioned the name of our dragoman.

Soon after, the lost member of our party came to us, and welcomed us cordially. He had been robbed by two men on his solitary ride, and had just induced the Bey of the village to send some soldiers in search of us. Our mules had rolled in a river, soaking our bedding so that it could not be used that night, and losing our wine. But such minor difficulties were only matters of amusement after our day of toils and perils. The Bey very courteously sent us a dinner from his own table, borne on trays on the heads of his servants, who waited on us in our tents, standing behind us, and making extempore spoons of the flat Arab bread, for us to dip in the dish, instead of civilized forks.

We had been in the saddle for thirteen nours. The alternate baying of shepherds' dogs and howling of wolves near our tents, could not prevent us sleeping soundly that night on our bare camp beds, wrapped up in shawls. The excitement of the day, however, did not wear off immediately, and it was some time before the pictures of Galilean scenery, rocky hills, wild wooded ravines, and shady forest paths festooned with fragrant flowers, which that day's fatigues had so imprinted on our minds, faded into dreams. We could not regret the mistake which had led us from the beaten track so far into the heart of Galilee.

XV.

Tyre.

FROM Bint-Jebail we turned again toward the sea coast. We were gradually leaving the Holy Land, yet the sacred chain of Bible memories seemed still to sweep forth into the secular history of Phœnicia, as the spurs of the Lebanon branch out into the strip of fertile lowland edged with golden sands which forms the Tyrian territory.

On Friday, July the 4th, after our day of thirteen hours of bewilderment and fatigue, we rested until nearly noon. Our road for many miles lay over a rich and picturesque mountain district, among evergreen trees and coppice, through green forest glades flickering with the July sunlight, which fell in burning flakes through the full dark foliage waving in the mountain breeze. The wild flowers were lovely, hiding like their shy English sisters amongst thick leaves in the shade, or glowing in masses of bright color, or festooning the trees; fragrant clematis, brilliant poppies, sweet familiar brier roses, delicate aristocratic cyclamens, and countless others that we could not stop to examine, and probably could not have named if we had.

It was a delightful, shady, varied, woodland ride, and in an hour or two we alighted for our midday meal in a pleasant dell shaded with thick trees and green with grass and herbage. Near us was a well, which supplied us and our horses with good cool water —and altogether, after the perplexities and toils of yesterday, we felt in luxurious ease. We had ample experience of the different effects of the same scenery, the same beauty, the same fatigues, when we know the port to which we are bound, and when we do not. In our heavenly pilgrimage we are not surely intended to experience any such weakening and perplexing doubts. Our warfare is not "uncertainly," not as one that "beateth the air." We know the enemy, the promised aid, the glorious end. Our pilgrimage should be made "not uncertainly." We know the Guide, and he knows the way and the better country to which he is leading us.

After our rest we rode for some time along a road (or a dry water course,) low in the valley, and piled with many layers of stones. On the brow of a hill above the coasts of Tyre, we passed what is called "the Tomb of Hiram," a massive, simple, square structure, consisting of a large plain stone sarcophagus, supported on a few gigantic hewn stones. This one name which links the history of Tyre in friendly and not corrupting association with that of Israel, made an interesting link between the land of promise we were leaving and the land of commercial greatness we were entering.

We encamped on the sandy hill outside the walls of modern Tyre. Wolfish-looking dogs, which belonged to no one, prowled about us, as usual, "outside" the "city." We kept one in pay by giving him the bones from our dinner table, and he was at once, [by the process adopted I believe in Greece,] transformed from a bandit to a police agent, conscientiously keeping off all his brethren from any share in his spoils.

Is it the influence of Christianity extending its law of kindness to the lower animals, or something in the nature of northern dogs and northern men, which makes dogs among us Anglo-Saxons, and all the associations connected with them, so entirely different from what they are in the East? Imagine the effigy of an Oriental saint reposing with its feet on a dog, like that of William the Silent, the heroic Prince of Orange, on the faithful spaniel which rescued his life in the night attack of the Spanish troops, and like so many a sculptured knight of mediæval times! The very presence of such an image would, in Oriental eyes, be the greatest desecration an enemy could inflict on a sacred edifice. And in the Bible how exceedingly contemptuous, and how inapplicable to civilized English dogs are the terms employed in describing canine habits: "They grin like a dog, and go about the city, and grudge if they be not satisfied"—"Outside are dogs." What possible resemblance is there between such a description and the grave dignity of a Newfoundland—the sagacious, acute expression of a terrier—the wistful, almost human eyes of our house spaniels? But here at Tyre, as in most Eastern towns, the familiar words came to us with all their true and forcible meaning. The wolfish, hungry, masterless dogs which "go about the cities," [of Alexandria, for instance] gathering in packs like jackals, prowling about for offal, and grudging if they be not satisfied, or the famished outcasts, like our dogs at Tyre, prowling outside the city—to these we may indeed apply the highly unfavorable definitions of Scripture; which every Englishman and Englishwoman must indignantly disclaim on behalf of the loyal, faithful, patient creatures who watch beside our homes like sentinels, and guard our flocks like shepherds, and welcome us with ecstatic joy when we come home again, and sometimes will even die rather than desert a master's grave.

The next day, Saturday, July the 5th, we went with an intelligent guide around Tyre. Our encampment on the sand hill was, we were told, nearly on the site of the earlier city, the Tyre which was "ancient Tyre" to the early Greeks. *That* Tyre has literally disappeared, and the dogs prowl, as I have said, on the "outside" sandy wastes, where once the queenly city stood

It was new (or island) Tyre, which Alexander converted into a peninsula by a causeway connecting it, which we explored that morning. This is a poor Turkish town, enlivened by a little faint commerce carried on in an easy Oriental way, in tobacco from the neighboring hills and in hard lava millstones transported from the volcanic districts of the Hauran to Tyre, as the sea-port for Egypt

We saw the ruinous cathedral, an edifice of the middle ages, with a spiral staircase—

and near it, inclined or prostrate, some fine columns of an earlier date with broken shafts and carved capitals. We afterwards took a boat, and skirted the bay from one tower of the fortifications to another on the opposite point of the island or peninsula. The most interesting ruins lay either close beside or beneath the waves. We passed a pier built of ancient columns, inserted at all angles—upright, reversed, leaning in various directions, half covered by the sea, or entirely exposed. We also noticed two ruined towers, with huge Phœnician-looking foundation-stones, which reminded us of those in the wall of the Temple enclosure at Jerusalem. But beneath the sea were the most impressive ruins of all. We looked far down through the clear, still water, and saw large granite columns lying there. Sea weeds and zoophytes had been clothing them for centuries, for millenniums, not knowing them from rocks. And to us their age seems more to be measured by geologic than by human dates.

After our ramble and boating expedition around the city, we rested and drank lemonade, iced with snow from Hermon! The associations of the place were bewildering, in the extent of time they covered, and the variety of race, religion, and civilization to which they point.

The prophetic doom of the great commercial power, and also of the queenly maritime city, has indeed been fulfilled, whether we regard it as referring to the ancient continental city, where now not a column stands nor a human being dwells, or to the clever, active, mercantile race, the founders of Carthage, which has passed away for ever from these shores. The doom was not on the buildings, but on the builders, or only on the buildings for the builders' sake. And yet if we regard only the external, visible stone city, rather than the luxurious, sin-laden, extinct human city, what more striking fulfilment of prophecy could we look for than that which meets our eyes here? The ancient Tyre is gone, literally razed from the face of the earth it polluted by its cruel idolatries and degraded social life.

The poor Turkish town which now stands in the place of island Tyre, is as little a continuation of the splendid city clothed with purple and scarlet, as the languid inhabitants—Syrian, Christian, or Metawali—are of that prosperous, energetic community, whose merchants were princes, and whose traffickers were the honorable of the earth.

The existence of this poor town near the site of Phœnician Tyre seemed to us to interfere as little with the fulfilment of the Scriptural denunciations, as if a similar doom had been pronounced on London, and, centuries after every Englishman had been swept from England, and every vestige of church, exchange, or dwelling had disappeared from the banks of the Thames, a colony of apathetic Hottentots were to build for themselves a village of half-excavated, half-thatched kraals on the wilds of Hampstead Heath.

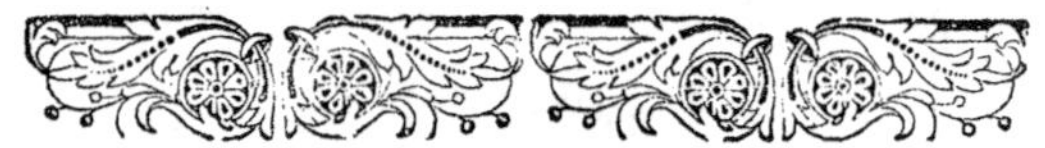

XVI.

The Shores of Tyre and Sidon,

THE LEBANON AND DAMASCUS.

ON Saturday, July 5th, we rode slowly along the Tyrian shore on our way across the Lebanon to Damascus.

We were no longer, strictly speaking, in the Holy Land; yet a little fragment of the Life whose history makes Palestine the Holy Land to the Christian, had been passed in this neighborhood. The feet whose tread had consecrated Judea and Galilee, once trod these shores of Tyre and Sidon.

We were outside the borders of the land of Israel. The rocky barrier of the promontory which breaks the long line of sandy shore between Gaza and the "Tyrian ladder," separated us from the land promised to

Abraham, and meted out by Joshua to the children of Abraham. Twice, however, the stream of Scripture history overflows that barrier; in two of the most affecting narratives of the Old Testament and of the New. These Tyrian shores, with all their magnificent memories of commercial greatness, are endeared to us by the names of two afflicted women, succored by the same merciful hand, —the widow of Sarepta and the woman of Canaan.

The story of the widow of Sarepta has an especial interest for us as one of the few facts selected by our Lord, from the earlier sacred history, to illustrate his own teaching. We have not only a divine history of the widow of Sarepta, but a divine commentary on it.

"But I tell you of a truth, many widows were in Israel in the days of Elias, when the heaven was shut up three years and six months, when great famine was throughout all the land; but unto none of them was Elias sent, save unto Sarepta, a city of Sidon, unto a woman that was a widow."

How remarkably the two narratives (of the Syrophœnician and the widow of Sarepta), display the same character in Him whose compassion they illustrate; in one through the instrumentality of the prophet, in the other manifest in the person of the Son. They are very precious to us as illustrating the unity of the moral theology of the Old Testament and the New. Amidst all the terrors of the old dispensation of law and judgment, we treasure up every indication which reveals the truth that in the thunders of Sinai, as in the dying cries of Calvary the voice is the same, and the foundation-tone of that voice is love;—love fencing off sin with barriers of unquenchable fire,—love drawing home the sinner with accents of unquenchable tenderness. The heart that was moved with compassion for the widow of Nain, and would not have the little children driven away, is the same which provided, with such minute care, that the gleaners, "the stranger, the fatherless, and the widow" should have the corners of the field and the forgotten sheaf left for them. He who sent the prophet with the unfailing cruse to the widow of Sarepta, chastened her into repentance by the death of her son, and then melted her into adoring gratitude by raising him from the dead;—is He not the same who, centuries afterwards, on the same shores, listened to the Canaanite in spite of the remonstrances of his disciples, proved her faith by delay, and then crowned it with that royal promise, "Be it unto thee even as thou wilt."

On the shore, not far from Tyre, we passed a very fine ancient reservoir, and crossed several streams of fresh, sweet water, whose springs are not more than a mile from the sea. They must have tended to make this coast populous. It was strange to think of the busy commercial life which once stirred along these desolate shores, of the countless sails which must have speckled this blue sea, sails of ships laden with the raw material of uncivilized Europe or Africa, or the wrought wares of the Phœnician colonies, with gold and spices from the south and east, or the useful metals from our own English mines. "Tarshish was thy merchant by reason of the multitude of all kind of riches; with silver, iron, tin, and lead, they traded in thy fairs." Seamen and miners (or native proprietors, perhaps), came hither from Marazion and other places in Cornwall, with the produce of the tin stream works, the pits of which now remain on the moors of Cornwall and Devonshire! Probably, indeed, the trade was carried on chiefly by the Phœnician colonists themselves, as ours is with New Zealand now, by our own ships and seamen; yet no doubt now and then an enterprising native of some West of England fishing-village came with the Phœnician crew, to help work the ship, and to gaze on the riches and splendor of that marvellous eastern world. For "the ships of Tarshish did sing of thee in thy markets." Often, perhaps along those shores, and from the walls of that grand old city resounded the wild melody of some Celtic ballad, sung by Cornish seamen as they heaved the anchor or toiled at the oar.

Along the very way we were going, mules had plodded from Damascus laden with wine-skins from the vineyards on the sunny slopes not then bared by Moslem law, and with white wool from the flocks of the Bedouins on the far reaches of the eastern desert. Whilst from the south, from the terraced hills and cultivated valleys of the desolate land amidst which we had been wandering, had journeyed long rows of mules and camels, carrying market-wheat, olive oil, honey and balm, the produce of Jewish olive groves, and corn-fields, and breezy thyme covered hills.

But as they pointed out to us some ruins on the slope of a hill on our right, and called them Surafend (that is, Sarepta), our thoughts quitted all these busy highways of trade to follow the solitary path of the prophet from the dried-up brook among the arid hills near Jericho, all through the parched and famine-smitten land, to this Sidonian city. How familiar the scene that rose before our minds! Those Celtic miners and Phœnician colonists seem distant and half mythical, like King Arthur and the Round Table; but the widow of Sarepta, who lived here in the same far-off ages, is as a friend of our earliest days. The wasted, stooping form, worn by grief and famine, gathering the few dry sticks on the parched ground by the city gate; the home from which she came, with its "loft" or upper chamber, its meal-barrel so nearly exhausted, and its oil-cruse so nearly empty—and the one child, the widow's only son;—how well we knew them all! Among those ruins on that hill-top, looking over the Mediterranean, that story was lived which has become so typical of man's need and God's providence to all time. The barrel of meal and the cruse of oil never containing more than the day's provision, yet always containing enough—what richer type does the Bible afford of God's supply of daily bread to his children?—"a daily rate for every day all the days of our life." And here, among those ruined walls, the actual, literal cruse and barrel stood, and were daily replenished by Divine care.

The precise scene of that other narrative whose locality is on these shores, is not told.

There was a home—a heathen home—on this coast once, where lived a mother and her young daughter. But between the mother and the child, and between that young maiden and peace and heaven, had intruded another inmate, desecrating all. "An unclean spirit" possessed the child; and of the anguish, the degradation, the separation implied in those words how little can we conceive! The most loathsome disease can but touch the body, but this impure and malignant spirit touched and soiled the maiden's soul.

Then came the rumor of the arrival of a mysterious Galilean in the land, whose power evil spirits acknowledged—"for He could not be hid." Mighty to heal and gracious to help in this world of hopeless and helpless need, how, indeed, could he be hid? The mother found him. And the rapid dialogue seems to echo along these shores, a lesson to all ages of what God means by delaying answers to prayer, and how infinitely more tender the Saviour's heart is to the suppliant than that of any disciple.

The cry of anguish—"Have mercy on me, O Lord, thou son of David; my daughter is grievously vexed with a devil!" But he answered her not a word. Strange silence on the lips usually only silent on his own sorrows, and so ready to speak words of pardon and peace! How she must have watched his countenance! But whatever *she* read there, the disciples read its expression wrong.

"Send her away," they said; "she crieth after us." *Us!* How soon Pharisaism creeps into the heart but just healed from its own self-condemning sorrow. These disciples, so lately called from the publican's seat, or the broken fish-nets—so lately crying, "Depart from me, a sinful man, O Lord!" —so soon to need faithful rebuke and tender intercession, and to prove all the depth of forgiveness in the heart they understood so little now. Happily for her, it was *not* "after *them*" she cried. But he answered and said (not to them, but to her), "I am not sent but unto the lost sheep of the house of Israel." The words had little encouragement. The look and tone must have explained them, for she was not repelled by them. "She came and" (attempting no argument) simply "worshipped him, saying, Lord, help me"—the best argument a needy human creature can use. She cast herself, helpless and needy, on his grace.

"But he answered and said, It is not meet to take the children's bread, and cast it to dogs."

Dogs! What words from his lips! She was of the human nature he had taken on him never more to lay it down—of that race he had come to redeem; yet she made no remonstrance. She was not, in the Jewish sense, "a child;" she admitted it. She had no claim to the privileges of the household—

no claim but her misery and His mercy. Crumbs must fall from that plentiful table, and he would not refuse them even to the "dogs."

Then was a change! The searching test was over. No more humbling epithets; but commendation to crown her through all time: "O woman, great is thy faith: be it unto thee even as thou wilt." There had been no limit to her humiliation and trust; there was no limit to his gift.

She went back to her house and found her child no longer roaming about hither and thither with the carelessness of insanity, or the restlessness of a lost spirit, but "laid on the bed," peacefully resting, and able to meet her mother's eyes with the conscious smile of recognition and love.

What intercourse must have followed between them!

Once more, however, the veil is drawn; and those two lives, one fragment of which stands out in such vivid light for us, are again withdrawn into the darkness.

Not thirty years afterwards, the apostle Paul "landed at Tyre," and, "finding disciples, tarried there seven days." "And when those days were accomplished, we departed and went our way; and they all brought us on our way, with wives and children, till we were out of the city; and we kneeled down on the shore and prayed. And when we had taken our leave, one of another, we took ship, and they returned home again."

They knelt together on these Tyrian sands, Jew and Gentile,—no more "dogs" and "children," but one family, God's one household. The disciples had learned much since that "Send her away."

Were the Syrophœnician, an aged gray-haired woman, and that restored daughter among that kneeling, weeping company? We cannot tell. It is enough service for one woman to render, to hand down with her memory from generation to generation, that one lesson of humility and trust, and of the unfailing answer to every faithful prayer, "Be it unto thee even as thou wilt."

This narrative of the Syrophœnician was the last association of gospel story which was to illuminate our Syrian journey, although the Tyrian shores were not the last spot we saw consecrated by a visible manifestation of the Saviour.

From the shore we wound up among the hills, crossing a river, which they told us was the Leontes, although there seemed some preplexity as to its connection with the Leontes, or Litany, which we meet again deeper in the heart of the mountains. We rode along a high rocky ledge of the hills, and then wound through a valley and by a high ridge to the village of Nebudiyeh, where we found our tents pitched in a harvest field.

It must have been on that day or the next that we noticed two customs which brought the words of the Bible to our recollection. One was an old man gathering dry grass for the oven. He unconsciously read us this parable, "Wherefore, if God so clothe the grass of the field, which to-day is, and to-morrow is cast into the oven, shall He not much more clothe you, O ye of little faith?"

The other incident recalled the story of Sisera. Weary and thirsty we reached a lonely farm among the mountains, and asked for a drink of water. The woman of the house (like so many mountaineers) was hospitable and friendly, and brought us some buttermilk instead of water. It was quite sour, but one of our party found it as refreshing as Sisera did, although not brought to us like that butter, or buttermilk of old, in a "lordly dish," but in a humble earthen bowl. We were told that in the hot weather the milk of the morning cannot be kept for the day.

In the evening, at Nebudiyeh, the brother of the governor came in state to welcome our party.

The next day, Sunday, was very grateful to us after our week's hard work. That Sunday among the mountains has left a recollection of deep peace and rest. The gentlemen of our party had necessarily to return the visit of the governor's brother, but I was too glad of repose, and too little inclined for any more visits to hareems, to accompany them. There was time, therefore, for a long quiet rest with the Bible for a companion, whilst a cool breeze occasionally stirred the folds of the tent. From time to time some of the peasant women peeped in to see their Frank sister, but usually they contented themselves with looking on from a distance, seated in picturesque groups about the field. Now and then the pleasant sound of bells fell on the ear from strings of camels passing, laden with corn, to the village, or returning unladen. In the afternoon we had a delightful walk up the hill behind our corn-field and sat reading the Bible in view of Mount Hermon.

Our dinner after sunset was attended by a large concourse of unbidden guests, besides the governor and his brother who sat at our table invited. The whole male population of the village apparently collected to see us dine, and seated themselves in a semi-circle outside our tent, observing us in a grave Oriental way; some of the older men smoking, and the women peeping round behind, wrapped in their white veils. It might have been embarrassing had the circle been less grave and reserved.

The gentlemen had previously partaken of an Oriental repast at the governor's house, where they observed one custom which illustrates many of the Bible narratives of feasts.

The repast was held in a room which any one seemed free to enter. A number of unbidden guests came in whilst they were eating, composedly seated themselves quite close to their divans, and occasionally joined in the conversation. It brought to our minds many a feast in the house of Pharisee and publican, at which evidently many were present unbidden, yet unforbidden, and not regarded as intruders.

On Monday we had a fatiguing mountain ride of ten hours, over indescribably hard roads, to a village which our guide called Ha-aroni. We were rewarded by two magnificent extensive mountain views; one from the summit of the first ridge we crossed, over a deep valley and many hills, to Hermon; the other from the summit of the second ridge, far into the depths of the Lebanon. In the early part of day we forded a stream bordered with a deep shubbery of luxuriant oleanders in full flower; and as we climbed the mountains we crossed many beautiful clear streams, gushing from the rocky sides of the hills, and traced them, as they flowed down the steep hill-sides, and through the valleys below, by the gardens of myrtle and oleander with which they bordered themselves. In some places our path lay through thickets of aromatic flowering myrtle.

We took our mid-day rest under the shade of a grove of fine old trees, by an abundant stream high on the mountains gushing from the rocks,—a river at its source, and cold as iced water. Afterwards we descended into a most beautiful garden of a valley; the sides clothed with fine sweeping fir trees, aromatic in the sunshine; and the bottom watered by a large rocky stream clear as crystal, flowing through a wilderness of oleanders and glossy-leaved myrtles, all in full flower. One large cluster of oleanders stood grouped in a meadow, as if by the hand of some skilful landscape gardener. It was literally "a fountain of gardens,—a well of living waters,—and streams from Lebanon." Our journey then became less interesting, the vegetation more ordinary. It seemed a descent from a region of romance into the everyday world, to find the streams once more bordered with homely rushes instead of glowing oleanders, and to pass through thickets of brambles and briar-roses in place of the thickets of fragrant myrtle, intsead of the fir-tree to find the thorn, and instead of the myrtle-tree the briar. From this little Eden like dell we climbed another mountain, and then rode along a broad, common-place valley between low hills, with a level outline, to a river we told was called the Kasimaya, close to which our tents were pitched for the night.

We sat in a corn-field near our encampment while our dinner was being prepared, watching the peasants making up the sheaves, until the golden evening sun-beams faded from the corn-sheaves, ceased to light up the the shepherds with their flocks crossing the ancient bridge or drinking of the river, and only lingered in a crimson glow on the snows of Hermon. At last even that died away, and the long back of the great, sacred old mountain couched heavy and dark against the sky, whilst beneath us flowed the river, eddying round a little rushy, reedy island below the bridge.

The incidents and scenery of the next day have not left quite so deep an impression on our memories as those of our first day on Lebanon. It was a fatiguing ride of more than eleven hours, for the most part through dreary arid hills. At mid-day we rested by an abundant spring, where flocks were being watered; and towards the evening, as we approached towards Khan Dimas, we rode through two very fine deep, craggy ravines or chasms, which reminded me of the Saxon Switzerland. Otherwise the day was chiefly one of endurance, of toiling steadily on with much fatigue and heat, through a lifeless, arid country.

On Wednesday the scenery was still more dreary, and the heat greater,—a long toil of many burning hours up and down parched, verdureless, sandy, desert hills. And then suddenly, from the brow of the last hill, burst on us, in indescribable contrast, the marvellous view of Damascus.

We had been enduring three days of most fatiguing travelling, and for six hours had been toiling over burnt-up, sandy hills, our eyes blinded by the glare, and almost fainting with the heat; not a blade of grass, or even a stunted green bush in sight; only thinly dotted here and there some leafless, stalky, dusty, sandy things, not to be called plants. And all at once, on reaching the brow of the hill, acres, miles, a sea of deep, dark green woods burst on our sight,—the richest, coolest green imaginable, contrasted with countless airy minarets, white and delicate as carved ivory. It was not the bright green of grass, but the deep, rich, soft green of woods, into which the wearied sight could plunge and lose itself, as in a deep sea of living coolness, And amongst all this were three rivers,—rivers which would be called rivers in the North,—flowing, splashing, abounding rivers. The voice of one of them came to our ears from the valley immediately below us. It is a forest of gardens—walnuts, mulberries, apples, oranges, lemons—every kind of tree that is pleasant to the eye and good for food.

In comparison with things unseen I can think of nothing like it, except when some trembling, toil-worn, doubting, desponding Christian, such as Cowper, wakes up on the brow of the last arid hill his fainting feet will ever have to climb, and sees before him paradise, and hears, "To-day thou shalt be with me."

XVII.

Damascus, Baalbec,

AND THE COAST OF ASIA MINOR.

DAMASCUS, *Friday*, July 11.

COMING from the Holy Land to Damascus is like stepping straight out of the Bible into the Arabian Nights. The heat is intense to-day, the thermometer 87 degrees in the shade, and 130 degrees in the sun, but in our rooms we are quite cool. Our hotel is a palace built by a great man among the Turks one hundred and twenty years ago. The saloon in which I am writing is forty or fifty feet high, with an arched roof. Through the open door I look on a court containing a large tank filled with running water, and shaded by a fine orange tree. In another corner of the court is a tall oleander in full bloom. The court is paved with inlaid marbles, and so is the saloon. In the room where I am sitting is a fountain or bath, octagonal in form, and made of rich marbles inlaid with mother-of-pearl, into which water is constantly flowing from two spouts—water not cool merely, but cold. On each of the three sides of this marble hall a high step leads into an arched alcove, the walls and arches of which are exquisitely painted in frescoes of Moorish design. One of these alcoves, the one opposite the door, has a divan, and niches with carved marble slabs, and cupboards with doors of richly carved and gilded wood. In this I am sitting. The other two alcoves are equally decorated, and curtained off with muslin drapery—they contain French beds.

The charm of Damascus is the abundant fresh, cold water in contrast with the intense heat. How such streams can spring out of the dry burnt up hills where they rise seems a mystery. Three fresh, cold, abundant rivers flow through the city. Water meets you everywhere in every form; in streams by the roadside; in conduits and drinking basins in the streets; in tanks, and baths, and flowing fountains in the houses. No wonder Naaman thought his rivers of Damascus better than all the waters of Israel!

On Friday we visited the bazaars and several palaces on the same model as our hotel, some of them very magnificent, with mosaics and frescoes of colors most exquisitely blended. The mosques we were not allowed to enter. It struck us that we had nowhere encountered such fierce and fanatical scowls from the Moslems as here.

On Saturday we rode to the junction of the Baradas and Banias—two of the rivers of Damascus—and visited some Roman ruins. The magnificence of the houses is all internal. Within, many of the palaces are the perfection of oriental beauty and luxury. Outside, they present nothing but dull windowless walls, often cased with mud, with only one narrow dark entrance.

On Sunday we had the English service in the saloon.

On Monday, July 14th, at half-past six, we left Damascus on our way across the Cœle Syrian plain and Lebanon to Beyrout. The scenery through which we rode on that and the following day was very varied and fine. At first we wound in and out among the hills by the side of the Baradas, one of the rivers of Damascus, an abounding vigorous mountain river, like our Devonshire rivers, but as abundant in this burning Syrian July as these are after the continuance of rain. It was a most delicious sight and sound. The road, as it wound up the hillside, was continually returning to the banks of the river as it foamed and dashed along in a series of cascades and rapids, now and then plunging over a precipice into a deep, dark pool below. By its side was a strip of the deepest green vegetation—poplars rising among rich groves of various trees, or from meadows green as alpine mountain pastures just unveiled from their winter snows. Above, in stern contrast, rose the unwatered hills, brown, bare, and lifeless. Our midday rest was under a tree by another stream, where we bought goat's milk from a friendly herd boy who was watering his flocks.

In the evening, after turning aside to see a fine water fall, we encamped at Zebdani in a beautiful rich, broad valley, dotted with many flourishing villages. On the height above us was perched the village of Bleudan. Our tents were pitched on a green meadow, watered by two or three springs of cold pure water.

On Tuesday our path lay again by streams and fountains, until, crossing the watershed of the Anti-Libanus, we came to another river flowing in an opposite direction, towards the Mediterranean, a pleasant sight for us westward-bound travellers. When we left this river, we and our guide lost our way among the hills, until, after wandering many weary hours, (we scarcely knew in what direction,) quite by surprise, across a reach of the Cœle Syrian plain, burst on our sight six enormous columns on a lofty pedestal of ruined masonry, the six characteristic columns of Baalbec. We entered the village, and were allowed to encamp within the ruins.

Palestine is not a land of ruins, but of ruinous heaps ; and the extent of these magnificent remains, with their perfect preservation in parts, amazed us. In the Holy Land the most interesting and sacred places are scarcely marked by a few poor scattered stones ; and here were ruined temples and dwellings worthy of the metropolis of an empire or the sanctuary of a religion. But the story was lacking ! With all this grandeur no human associations are linked—no great name of man or nation is bound up with the e wonderful walls. What the eye saw was grand beyond anything we had seen,—but what the eye saw was all. It is useless to describe what drawing and description have made so familiar to us, and yet what neither drawing nor description can give any adequate idea of. It seemed to us more like a city of temples than one temple; and very solemn it was to sit still and see the gigantic shadows of the one almost perfect temple, and of the six grand columns remaining of another thrown across the great moonlit spaces of the courts, broken only here and there by enormous sculptured blocks, the remains of capital and fallen shaft.

On the next morning (Wednesday) we walked round the ruins, inside and outside, wondering at the size of the stones, and admiring the beauty of the proportions, and especially the broken doorway of the most perfect temple. The enormous mass of masonry on which these temples stand rises more like a hill than a building from the great Cœle-Syrian plain; and the vaults which lead through it look more like tunnels excavated through a mountain than blocks laboriously piled, as they must have been, one on another by human hands. We measured some stones fifty feet long. We lingered some time longer in the courts of the temple and particularly by that broken porch, with its deeply sculptured roof, and the staircase beside it winding up through the wall. There was so much delicate work, such an extent and number of buildings to examine, that we found it difficult to leave; and yet before nightfall we must reach those hills whose outline lay so blue and faint against the sky, across the great plain.

We started a little after mid-day, and reached the mountains by sunset, after a ride of five hours, much of it at a gallop across the level. On our way we passed the quarry out of which Baalbec was hewn, and observed one gigantic block like that we had measured in the temple. Why was it, we asked ourselves, that this fragment of unfinished work impressed us more, and seemed to bring the past nearer than all the marvellous finished structures we had been surveying in the morning? Was it not because in such interrupted work you seem to read the past, not in the perfect but the present tense; in the active, not in the passive voice; not in its stately monumental repose, but in its actual everyday toil? How was that block brought so far? Why was it brought no further? What silenced that noisy work-place and scattered the workmen? That one stone in the quarry of Baalbec seemed to bring us more into the presence of the living men of its past generations, and stir our minds with more speculation as to their history than all its magnificent temples.

After this I remember no incident for the day, but only a swift galloping or a steady toiling across the burning plain, and noticing from time to time the lizards creep in and out under the shadow of the stones, brown as their hiding-places, taking literally (as we all do more or less, figuratively), the color of their homes.

We encamped for the night by a stream near the Christian (Maronite) village of Zabbi. It was strangely familiar to hear once more the sound of a church bell, from the village church.

Our ride on Thursday, July the 27th, was through very fine mountain scenery, and along most perilous roads, or rather no roads. The paths seemed to us steeper, more slippery, and rougher than any we had yet traversed. Besides the fact of no road ever being made or repaired, common to all Syria, the mountaineers of Lebanon have a perplexing custom of throwing all the large stones which they clear out of their vineyards on the pathway outside. We had become habituated to regarding the dry beds of torrents in the light of high roads; but on this part of the Lebanon, in several places, our paths lay along actual flowing torrents, and up and down cascades. How the horses ascended and descended safely over those slabs of rock, polished and actually covered by flowing water, is beyond explanation. But, if you trust them, these little Syrian horses will scramble successfully over anything; the only danger is, lest in a nervous apprehension you attempt to guide them, and so check the freedom of their movements, on which your safety depends. It is a greater wonder, still, how the heavily laden pack mules accomplish the journey; for this is the trading highway between Damascus and Beyrout, and yet, we were told, accidents are very rare.

Our rest in the hotel at Beyrout was very welcome to us, but we could not part without regret from the little patient horses which had carried us so bravely through many a toilsome mile. One consideration, however, helped to reconcile us. We were glad to have the prospect of travelling by means of machines, steamboats and trains, which the reckless carelessness and lazy indifference of Syrian muleteers could not hurt or distress. All our horses had sores, from the rubbing of saddles or packs when we started, which a little care soon healed; but one mare—a willing, faithful creature—died at Damascus, in consequence of bad shoeing and the over-driving of the obstinate Mukris. I shall never forget the mute appealing look of that poor brown mare, as they drove her with her wounded feet over the stones towards me; nor how forcibly it brought to my heart the words, "The whole creation groaneth and travaileth in pain together until now, waiting for the adoption, to wit the redemption of the body."

We had rooms in the "Hotel de Bellevue," outside Beyrout, the provisional master of which, at the time, (under its widowed mistress) was Dmitri Karas, formerly dragoman to the author of "Eothan."

Friday and Saturday were spent in rest, *keff*, bathing, and sketching. From the broad roofed corridor of the hotel, at each end, we had most exquisite views; at one end, of the sea and hills; at the other of the beautiful blue expanse of the harbor of Beyrout, with the flat-roofed white houses relieved against the great mass of the Lebanon, which rose behind them in a grand sweep, from the sea to the clouds and the eternal snow.

Below us were two cottages, half hidden among orchards and gardens, with open wooden balconies. They were inhabited, the American consul told us, by two widows, a mother-in-law, and a daughter-in-law, both bereaved not long before by the cholera, and in great poverty, which it was a pleasure to all in the hotel to contribute a little to relieve. The consul told us how terrible it was, during the time of the cholera, to hear from that corridor the dreadful hopeless death - wails bursting from house after house.

We had to wait some days in the hotel for the French steamer. The views from our corridor during that time, of the sunsets over the Mediterranean, have left a deep impression on our minds. The after-glow, when the sun had set, was so beautiful; and then we seemed to see Night like a visible Presence slowly advancing and spreading her wings over the water.

On Tuesday, July 22d, we embarked in the French steamer, for our coasting voyage by Asia Minor to Constantinople.

We were not allowed to land anywhere until we came to Rhodes, on account of the fever then prevailing on the coast. But we had ample opportunities for observing the coast during the many hours the vessel lay off the various ports. Those little white towns on the narrow levels near the sea, at the base of the great mountain ranges, are the natural homes of fever, in such a climate.

On Wednesday, we lay some hours off Latakia, of tobacco celebrity, and Tripoli, the last place the Crusaders held on the Asiatic shores, which looked very picturesque with its white houses, and ruined towers, relieved against a background of wooded mountains.

On Friday, we spent some hours in sight of Mersina, once the port of Tarsus. Beyond that range of volcanic conical hills, with truncated summits, cleft by rugged chasms, and broken into fantastic crags, lay the home of our own apostle, the Apostle of the Gentiles. Through that ravine which cleft the mountains, just behind the town of Mersina, he had doubtless journeyed again and again. And by these shores had coasted, with his heart full of the infant Churches he had founded in the sea port towns, or among the mountains.

Much of the coast, especially near Cape Khelidoni, struck us as extremely fine in outline; the forms of the hills so bold and varied.

At Rhodes, we landed and spent some hours in exploring the fortifications and the city. It was interesting, after seeing the final seat of the Knights of St. John at Malta, and the ruinous building opposite the Church of the Holy Sepulchre at Jerusalem which gave them their title of the Knights Hospitallers, to visit the fertile island where they reigned so proudly as the Knights of Rhodes.

On the whole, the Turks are satisfactory keepers of ruins, when only the picturesque is regarded; because, if they have not energy to repair, neither have they enterprise to alter. Thus, in the streets of Rhodes you can recall the old inhabitants with little effort of imagination. Their dwellings and fortifications are too strongly built for time, in this pure, dry air, to have had much power over them. The city is full of relics of the knights. The street architecture strongly resembles that of Malta. Projecting balconies, roofed in with lattices, as at Valetta; beautiful carved mouldings and coats of arms, cut in imperishable stone, each line as sharp, and each edge as white and fresh, as when the sculptor's chisel left it four centuries ago. We went up the silent street of the knights, and into the houses of the different "languages," still marked by their characteristic armorial bearings—the fleur de lys, the lion, or the papal keys; and unforbidden we rambled around the ancient fortifications, saw the cannons of the knights, left after the siege; the three moats, the three walls, the drawbridges,—mediæval Christian word, all now in Moslem hands. The arches and walls were very solid, and the mouldings beautifully delicate. The favorite device seemed to be a twisted rope. We were permitted, without difficulty, to enter the old cathedral, now transformed into a mosque by the simple process of adding to the altar-steps, so as to make them front towards Mecca, in a line diagonal to the walls, and covering them with prayer-mats and Persian rugs. The fine granite columns are plastered over, and the Mohammedan's abhorrence against idolatry has been appeased by mutilating or removing the faces of the knightly effigies, which still lie headless on the walls. The Mohammedanism which is so fanatical and fierce in Damascus and other cities of the East, seems merely to lie like a dull, dead weight on Rhodes, shrouding it with that peculiar silence characteristic of Moslem cities; the silence of cities in which there are no homes and no churches, and in which the women creep about in black or white veils, like shrouded ghosts, afraid of daylight.

The two harbors are fine, but too shallow for modern ships of war. Long after we had re-embarked, and had passed Rhodes, the white towers of the old Christian fortifications gleamed across the deep blue of the sea.

Early at break of day on the morning after leaving Rhodes, we were called on deck to see the shores of Patmos. The sun was rising behind the island, and strongly relieving against the golden sky, the long, bare, hard outline of its crags, crowned by the line of the monastery, in a cave beneath which (tradition says) St. John lived during his banishment. It was most interesting to stand silently on the deck, and watch the sun rise behind the rocks on which the last vision of heavenly glory was vouchsafed to mortal eyes; where the Apocalypse was beheld, and the whole Book of Revelation solemnly closed.

Several small islands, or isolated rocks, stand near Patmos, which looked very beautiful in the morning light.

These Greek islands were a fairy-land of beauty at sunrise and sunset, reminding me of that story of our childhood, of the child's journey into the fairy country, where one palace was of topaz, another of porphyry, another of ruby, another of gold or pearl. As we passed in and out among them, one island rose behind another from the deep blue sea with the most exquisite variety of tints and forms; the warm glow of sunset on some of the peaks, and on others the loveliest delicate greys, fading into pearl in the distance. All hues were there,—glowing, blushing, golden violet, opal, grey; and all varieties of beautiful outlines,—soft, curved, bold, angular,—blended as in the curves and angles of Greek carving; whilst between them glided in and out the white sails of the Greek fishing-boats, with their picturesque curves, like the spread wings of birds. We felt we were entering the home of the race to whom it was given to interpret the beauty of God's world to other men.

The shores of these islands, when you come close to them, are for the most part mere barren crags; but the forms and colors, especially at evening and morning, are most enchanting. It is as if the sea had inundated a magnificent mountain chain, the peaks of which are converted into islands, and its rich plains and valleys into a plain of blue heaving waters.

In the interior, they say, some of these islands are fertile; but the war of the Greek revolution has depopulated them sadly; and nothing can ever revive under Turkish rule. Scio has many green spots on it, and houses are visible here and there from the sea; but, we were told, the Turkish massacres had reduced the population from one hundred and ten thousand to eight thousand.

On July the 19th our way lay still on and on among the Greek islands, and by the mountainous shores of Asia Minor, until we rounded a headland and found ourselves in the Bay of Smyrna. As we approached the bay the coasts of Asia became more green. Little villages appeared nestling in the clefts of the rocks, their white roofs contrasting with the cypress groves in which they were embosomed, while beneath stretched green terraces and slopes.

The bay of Smyrna is very fine in its deep, broad expanse, with the varied outline of its mountain sheres here and there clothed with wood (which looked luxuriant after the craggy Greek islands), and dotted with villages either level with the shores among the cypresses, or guarding the terraced vineyards on the hills. The town of Smyrna at the head of the bay is very picturesque from the sea, with its large groves of fine cypresses breaking the white clusters of houses which climb the hill, crowned by the old Genoese castle.

We were glad to land; and on Wednesday we rode on donkeys to the summit of the hill where the Genoese castle commands the town and bay. Below us lay a fertile valley, watered by a river whose windings we could trace for many miles. It was twice crossed by the arches of a ruined Roman aqueduct. How characteristic the ruins left by the Greeks and Romans are! The exquisitely proportioned temple or the amphitheatre of the Greek cities; the massive aqueduct and bridge, or the imperishable road of the Romans, how expressive they are of the races whose several dominant ideas seem to have been beauty and power.

A memory far more distant in time, here came near to our hearts—To the Church, the living, believing Church of this city of Smyrna, the Divine Epistle was addressed, not from apostle or evangelist, but direct from Him who liveth, was dead, and behold he is alive for evermore.

"And unto the angel of the Church of Smyrna write; These things saith the First and the Last, which was dead, and is alive; I know thy works, and tribulation, and poverty (but thou art rich), and I know the blasphemy of them which say they are Jews, and are not, but are the synagogue of Satan. Fear none of those things which thou shalt suffer: behold the devil shall cast some of you into prison, that ye may be tried; and ye shall have tribulation ten days: be thou faithful unto death, and I will give thee a crown of life."

And here, in the next century, Polycarp was faithful unto death, and has received, (although, indeed, *not* here) the crown of life.

Smyrna was the last place we visited, which is distinctly and definitely mentioned in the Bible. On account of the unsettled state of Greece at that time we did not land at Athens or Corinth. But even in Smyrna, Athens, and Corinth the associations are interesting to us, not on account of their dissimilarity from our ordinary life, but of their resemblance to it. We are entering the region, not of visible divine manifestations, but of Church history, although of Church history written by divinely inspired men. Here, therefore, the narrative of our Wanderings over Bible Lands and Seas may naturally end.

www.ingramcontent.com/pod-product-compliance
Lightning Source LLC
LaVergne TN
LVHW011158110826
845150LV00006B/1257

* 9 7 8 1 4 2 5 5 4 6 4 3 4 *